KUMON READING WORKBOOKS

6

Reading

Table of Contents

KUMON

Vocabulary
Treasure in Town 1

Date   /   /

Name

Level ☆

Score   /100

---

1 Read the following passage. Then answer the questions below.

Ava's hand slammed down on the button of her alarm clock a few seconds before it was supposed to ring. True, the volume was set as low as it could go, but Ava was not taking chances on anyone else waking up. She wasn't ready to tell anyone about her discovery until she was certain. Ava quietly reached into the bottom drawer of her dresser. She smiled at the thought that today all of this ①_____ might be over.

Who would have guessed that the maple tree in her backyard would be the ②_____ where an adventure would begin? Last week, while taking a soil sample for biology class, Ava had dug up the box that was now hidden under her socks in one of her drawers. The writing on the paper inside the box was mostly ③_____, but there was one letter that she was certain of. That letter was an "x," and it was drawn above a box with a heavy lock. Could the paper really be what she thought it was?

Ava raced downtown on her bike. She had made an appointment with the one person in town who she thought could help, and she did not want to be late. When Ava arrived at the town's only ④_____ shop, she told the owner, Mrs. Brown, about finding the paper buried next to the maple tree. Mrs. Brown ⑤_____ the paper for nearly an hour.

Finally, she shook her head in disbelief. "Ava," she said, "It's true. I think what you have here is a ⑥_____ treasure map."

---

(1) Complete the passage using the vocabulary words defined below.

5 points per question

genuine	actual or real; true
illegible	unreadable
inspected	reviewed or examined very carefully
antique	an object made at an earlier time (at least 100 years ago)
site	place or location
secrecy	the practice of keeping secrets or hiding information

---

(2) Answer the questions below using words taken directly from the passage.

10 points per question

① Why did Ava shut her alarm off quickly?

Ava shut her alarm off quickly because she was not _____

_____ .

② Why did Ava make an appointment with Mrs. Brown?

Ava made an appointment with Mrs. Brown because she was the one _____

_____ .

Read the passage. Then answer the questions below using words from the passage.

10 points per question

"It's the real thing, alright," said Mrs. Brown. "And somewhere in this room I have the key to the box on that map!" Ava watched with curiosity as Mrs. Brown inspected the contents of every drawer in the shop. Finally, Mrs. Brown opened a cabinet and pulled out a small box. "Aha," she exclaimed, handing the box to Ava. Ava opened it to find a beautiful old key.

"The last owners of your house sold me this key a long time ago. They told me that their grandfather was a very wealthy man who had left town to travel the world. He wanted to be sure his valuables would be safe for him if he returned home. He told his family he had locked up blocks of gold inside that same box that the key would open, but the hiding spot was a matter of secrecy. I didn't think the story was genuine, but the key was so pretty that I let them think I believed it."

Mrs. Brown agreed with Ava that the writing on the map was illegible, but she was able to guess that the spot marked with an "x" was somewhere on the trails next to the river. The grandfather must have made the map to remind himself where he had buried the box. Mrs. Brown and Ava spent the day walking through the trails and finally arrived at the site marked on the map. "I think this is it," said Mrs. Brown. "Now we have to figure out how to dig up a heavy box filled with gold!"

(1) What did Ava watch Mrs. Brown do?

Ava watched with curiosity as Mrs. Brown _____

_____ in the shop.

(2) Why didn't the grandfather's family know where the treasure was hidden?

The grandfather's family did not know where the treasure was hidden because the hiding spot

was _____.

(3) What did Mrs. Brown think about the story the family told her?

She didn't think _____.

(4) What did Ava and Mrs. Brown think about the writing on the map?

They thought that the writing _____.

(5) How did Mrs. Brown and Ava arrive at the site marked on the map?

Mrs. Brown and Ava spent _____

_____ arrived at the site marked on the map.

I wouldn't mind finding some buried treasure!

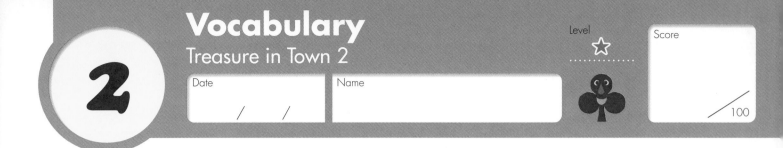

Vocabulary
Treasure in Town 2

Date   /   /

Name

Level

Score

/100

1   Read the following passage. Then answer the questions below.

"I hadn't even thought about that," said Ava with a laugh. "Neither did I," said Mrs. Brown. "I was so excited about our adventure that I hadn't planned a general ①_____ for getting the treasure out of the ground. You know, now that I think about it, these trails belong to the town. There are probably town ②_____ about digging that we have to think about. It's not as if we can just dig up the ground and take the treasure. It's even possible that the treasure might belong to the town now, too. We don't want to be accused of ③_____ treasure off of public property!"

The two sat on a rock in the shade of a nearby maple tree to ④_____ the situation.

The more they talked, the more it became clear that this treasure hunt wasn't so simple. Mrs. Brown worried that even though she owned the key, the treasure might belong to the town and not Ava. Maybe it still belonged to the man's family. "Well, I guess we have a lot to think about," said Ava. "To start with, we're going to need a pulley or some sort of ⑤_____ to lift the box out of the ground once we reach it, and that's not something we can keep a secret from everyone in town. We're probably going to need some help with it, too, especially if we don't want to hurt any nearby plants when we dig."

"Well, one thing I'm certain of," said Mrs. Brown, "is that 'x' marks the spot. This maple tree we're sitting under looks just like the one on the map."

(1)   Complete the passage using the vocabulary words defined below.   6 points per question

consider	to think about deeply or carefully
mechanism	a machine or system used for a task
regulations	formal rules or laws, often very detailed
smuggling	taking or moving something secretly and illegally
strategy	a plan made to achieve a goal

(2)   Answer the questions below using words taken directly from the passage.   10 points per question

①   To whom did Mrs. Brown say the trails belong?

Mrs. Brown said the trails belonged _____.

②   Where did Ava and Mrs. Brown sit to consider the situation?

The two sat _____ of a nearby maple tree.

③   Even though Mrs. Brown owned the key, what did she worry about?

Mrs. Brown worried that the treasure _____ and

not Ava.

Read the passage. Then answer the questions below using words from the passage.

10 points per question

"You know what? That tree looks a lot like the maple tree in my yard where I found the map," Ava exclaimed. "That was probably another way the man thought to remind himself of where he buried the box." Ava looked at the map and then she considered the spot on the ground next to the tree. "Mrs. Brown, I think the grandfather knew he wasn't coming back home. He wanted someone else to find that treasure. And that's going to be us!"

Mrs. Brown smiled. "I think the story behind this interests you more than the treasure itself, and that's something I can understand. I like to think that every object I sell in my shop has a story behind it." The two decided to come up with a strategy to dig up the buried treasure. Mrs. Brown said she would start by finding out whom the treasure actually belonged to. They also agreed that Ava would tell her biology teacher about the treasure. This way, they could learn about the town's regulations for the river's trails.

Ava's teacher explained to the class that the rules about digging in the park were created to keep people from harming plant life or smuggling protected wildlife away from the trails. That inspired Ava's class to come up with a mechanism that could carry up the box of treasure without harming any of the nearby plants.

It wasn't long before the whole town was involved in the treasure hunt. Of course, people disagreed about whether there was really any treasure under the maple tree, but as Ava said, there was only one way to find out!

(1) Why did Ava and Mrs. Brown need to think of a strategy?

They needed to come up with a strategy _____.

(2) Why did Ava tell her biology teacher about the treasure?

Ava told her biology teacher about the treasure so that they could _____

_____ for the river's trails.

(3) What did the rules prevent people from smuggling away from the river's trails?

The rules kept people from _____
the river's trails.

(4) What did Ava's biology class create to lift up the buried treasure?

They came up with a _____

_____ without _____.

Treasure hunting can get complicated!

5

Vocabulary
Dancing Puppets

3

Level ☆

Date / /

Name

Score /100

1 Read the following passage. Then answer the questions below.

An excited whisper filled the auditorium. The first act of the In Air Ballet Troupe's dance show was about to begin. The In Air Ballet Troupe was a talented dance group known for using a ①_____ of ballet and acrobatics in their performances. Tonight, for the first time, two puppets would dance along with the troupe in the second act. Everyone in the audience agreed that this should be very interesting to see.

The crowd's whisper turned to silence as the curtain opened. Several ballerinas twirled across the stage and were lifted into the air by other dancers. Their partners lifted them so high that it seemed as if the ballerinas were made of air. One of the ballerinas then performed a ②_____ backflip from her partner's shoulders. The backflip was so well done that it made the audience gasp and cheer in their seats! Two other dancers twirled on one foot for what seemed like several minutes. It seemed impossible that they could spin for so long without becoming dizzy, but they never lost their balance.

The troupe used their skilled dancing to ③_____ stories without using words. In the final dance of the first act, a group of guests watched the wedding of two of the dancers. After the ceremony of ④_____ had finished, the guests leapt into the air, performing a ⑤_____ dance in celebration.

The audience clapped loudly as the curtain closed on the first act. Everyone agreed that these dancers were talented and skilled. No one could have guessed that the In Air Ballet Troupe's big night was about to be spoiled by an ⑥_____ puppeteer.

(1) Complete the passage using the vocabulary words defined below.　　　5 points per question

combination	a group of things mixed or blended together
convey	to communicate or express meaning or feelings
incompetent	not having the skills to perform a task
jovial	happy and lighthearted; merry
matrimony	marriage
superb	excellent, outstanding

(2) Answer the questions below using words taken directly from the passage.　　　10 points per question

① What would happen for the first time tonight?

Tonight, for the first time, _____

_____ in the second act.

② Why did it seem like the ballerinas were made of air?

The ballerinas seemed like they were made of air because their _____

_____.

2 Read the passage. Then answer the questions below using words from the passage.

The audience applauded loudly as the curtain opened for the beginning of the second act. The dancing continued to be superb, much to the audience's delight. When the two puppets were lowered from the ceiling, the crowd conveyed its amazement with gasps and applause. The puppets were the size of people and looked much like real ballerinas with beautiful costumes.

At first it seemed like nothing was really wrong. One of the puppets bumped into a dancer, who pretended as if the bump was part of the act and performed a jovial leap in response. The audience laughed loudly. But it was soon clear that these puppets could not dance at all. Worried murmurs were heard in the audience as the clumsy puppets continued to bump into the dancers. The curtain was finally lowered when a group of ballerinas became entangled in the puppets' strings.

The incompetent puppeteer was not asked to perform again with the In Air Ballet Troupe. The troupe decided to stick with only real dancers in the future. The puppeteer decided she needed more practice to prevent any future disasters.

Later, those in the audience disagreed on the cause of the problem. Some said that it is very difficult for a puppeteer to learn ballet, while others said it was difficult for a puppeteer to learn acrobatics. Still others thought that the puppeteer was just not very good. A final group felt it was a combination of all three reasons. However, all of the people in the audience that night agreed on one thing: they had seen a performance they were unlikely to forget!

(1) Why was the audience delighted at the beginning of the second act?

The audience was delighted because the _____.

(2) How did the crowd express its amazement at the puppets?

When the two puppets were lowered from the ceiling, _____

_____.

(3) Why did the audience laugh at the dancer?

The audience laughed at the dancer because she pretended as if the puppet bumping into her

was _____ and performed _____

_____.

(4) Who was not asked to perform again with the troupe?

_____ was not asked to perform again with the In

Air Ballet Troupe.

(5) Different people in the audience thought that the puppeteer was incompetent for three different reasons. What did the last group think?

The last group thought it was _____

_____.

Do you like ballet?

Vocabulary
Caves and Caverns

Date / /

Name

Level ☆

Score /100

1 Read the following passage. Then answer the questions below.

    ① _____ are natural underground spaces that fascinate scientists, researchers, and everyday explorers. Long before apartment buildings and houses existed, many humans lived in such spaces. People who lived in caverns were safe from the wind, rain, and snow. When it got too hot or cold outside, the temperature inside these caverns was often still comfortable. Today, you probably don't live in a cavern, but you can still visit them in many places, including the United States.

    Caverns can be created in several ways, but most are formed when water mixes with an acid. This causes rock, such as ② _____, to crack. The water drips through the ③ _____ in the rock, making the space wider over a long time. The dripping water forms ④ _____ streams and rivers. When the water dries out, a cave is left.

    Researchers today study the pictures drawn on the walls of caves. This helps them learn about the life of prehistoric man. They may also find fossils and remains of prehistoric humans and other life. Scientists study interesting rock ⑤ _____ inside caves. They even study cave bacteria to understand how life might survive in similar habitats on other planets.

    A trip to a cave can be a chance for exciting exploration. You can visit Mammoth Cave in Kentucky to see the longest group of caves in the world — over 350 miles! The largest crystals on earth are inside the Crystal Cave of Giants in Mexico, but the high temperatures make it too ⑥ _____ for the average visitor to explore. It is so hot that scientists can only stay inside for a half hour at a time!

(1) Complete the passage using the vocabulary words defined below.   5 points per question

limestone	a common rock made mostly of sea shells
cavern(s)	naturally formed large cave, usually underground
crevice(s)	a very thin crack or a long, thin space
formation(s)	arrangement
subterranean	underground
treacherous	dangerous

(2) Answer the questions below using words taken directly from the passage.   15 points per question

  ① Why do researchers study pictures on the walls of caves?

    Researchers study them because they want to learn _____

    _____.

  ② What is inside the Crystal Cave of Giants?

    The largest _____ the Crystal Cave of Giants in Mexico.

2 Read the passage. Then answer the questions below using words from the passage.

10 points per question

There is an amazing variety of caverns on our planet. Some are filled with ice, some are filled with dirt, and some caverns are even filled with water. There are not just underground caverns — there are caverns under the sea, too.

One of the most well-known underwater caverns is the Great Blue Hole in the Caribbean Sea. The Great Blue Hole is the largest of its kind in the world and was first made famous by the nautical explorer Jacques Cousteau. He took his ship, the Calypso, to the Great Blue Hole to look at the formations on the walls. Afterwards, he showed the inside of the Great Blue Hole on his television show.

A blue hole is often called a vertical cave because it is a hole that drops straight down into the sea. When seen from above, the saltwater inside the hole is a very deep blue compared to the fresh water around it. Blue holes can be very treacherous places for divers to explore. One reason is that it can be difficult to see in such deep water. There can also be poisonous gases inside a blue hole.

Despite these challenges, the Great Blue Hole is a famous diving spot. A diver can explore the mysteries of the sea and experience an above-sea cave at the same time. That is because the Great Blue Hole was not always underwater! The Great Blue Hole is the opening to a large group of underwater caves. During the Ice Age, these caves were subterranean and were made of limestone, but they were still above the sea. When the ice melted, the sea levels rose and the caves became submerged underwater.

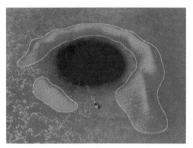

(1) What did Jacques Cousteau look at in the Great Blue Hole?

Cousteau took the Calypso to look at _____ cave walls.

(2) Why is a blue hole often called a vertical cave?

A blue hole is often called a vertical cave because _____

_____.

(3) Why are blue holes treacherous places for divers to explore?

Blue holes are treacherous places for divers to explore because seeing can be _____

in such deep water, and there can also be _____ inside.

(4) What were the caves connected to the Great Blue Hole like during the Ice Age?

During the Ice Age, the caves connected to the Great Blue Hole were _____

and were made of _____ but they were still _____.

I never knew caves were so interesting!

Vocabulary Review

5

Level ☆

Date / /

Name

Score
/100

1 Pick the correct word from the box to complete each sentence below.

5 points per question

| nautical | crevices | formations | combination | incompetent | genuine |

(1) The _____ of salty and sweet tastes makes kettle corn my favorite dessert.

(2) The crumbs from the open bag of cookies got into all of the _____ in the back seat.

(3) He explained nicely that he didn't fly planes, but that he was a _____ captain.

(4) The signature on Jamie's baseball card was declared _____ at the card shop.

(5) Leslie patiently learned all of the acrobatic _____ for the cheerleading team.

(6) The _____ accountant made too many mistakes.

2 Read the sentences. Then choose a word from each sentence to match each definition below.

5 points per question

--We went over to our neighbors' house to convey our happiness about the good news.

--My uncle's handwriting is almost illegible.

--"Once you consider the cost," she said, "maybe buying this is not a good idea."

--Mrs. Noelle lost many of her valuables in the fire.

--Race car driving can be a treacherous sport at times.

--We devised a mechanism that started the toaster when the alarm went off in the morning.

(1) _____ to think about deeply or carefully

(2) _____ unreadable

(3) _____ dangerous

(4) _____ articles of considerable value

(5) _____ to communicate or express meaning or feelings

(6) _____ a machine or system used for a task

3 Complete the crossword puzzle using the sentences below as clues. Use capital letters.

5 points per question

ACROSS

(1) We picked Jim to play Santa in the school play because he was always so ___?___.

(2) Chan always treated the cave as his ___?___ hideout.

(3) Anne had a little ceremony and joined her two cats in ___?___.

(4) The illegal ___?___ operation moved valuable metals out of the country daily.

(5) The winning team had a great ___?___ for scoring goals.

DOWN

(6) The list of ___?___ when it came to building a new house was very long.

(7) Our penny candy store has a large ___?___ of candies.

(8) Uncle Ron was upset with me when he found out I broke the ___?___ vase.

If you need a hint, try looking back at the previous pages!

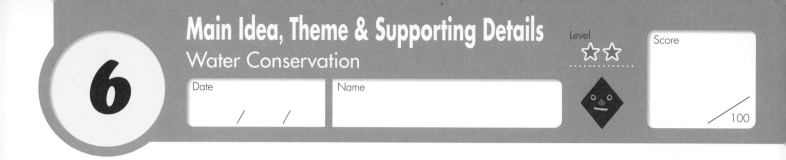

Main Idea, Theme & Supporting Details
Water Conservation

Level ☆☆

Score /100

Date / /

Name

1 Read the passage. Then answer the questions below.

> **A.** You have probably heard that we need to conserve water, but do you know why? Water is one of the most important substances on earth. Animals and plants both need water to live. A person cannot live without drinking water. This is not surprising, since the human body is over 70 percent water! In fact, besides air, water is the most important thing humans need to survive.
>
> **B.** Most of the earth is covered in water, but if we don't plan well, there may not be enough to go around in the future. Less than one percent of the water on earth is a good source of drinking water, so we only have a limited supply. Humans and many other living things need fresh water to survive, but most of the water on earth is in the ocean, which is saltwater. The remaining water is fresh water, but most of this fresh water is frozen in glaciers or ice caps. That doesn't leave much usable water!
>
> **C.** Without proper planning, droughts may become a worldwide problem in the future. The main reason for this is population growth. The number of people on earth is growing very quickly, and so is our need for water, but the earth does not create new water. We can only use the water we have, and it takes time for water to move back to us through the water cycle after it is used.
>
> **D.** Population growth also puts our water supply in peril for another reason. More people means more water pollution, and it is very important that the water we use is clean. People and other living things can often become very sick from polluted water.

(1) Complete the chart below showing the main idea and supporting details of the passage.

6 points per question

Main Idea	We need to ①_____.
Supporting Details	Water is one of the ②_____ on earth.
	We only have a ③_____ of water.
	④_____ may become a problem if we don't plan.
	⑤_____ water can make living things very sick.

(2) Match each title to the letter of the paragraph it best fits.

20 points for completion

① More People, More Pollution ( )

② More People, Less Water ( )

③ Life Needs Water ( )

④ The Limited Water Supply ( )

2 Read the passage. Then answer the questions below.

> **A.** Using too much water or throwing trash into our rivers are clear ways that humans can put our water supply in peril, but we also affect our water supply in less obvious ways. You may wonder how paving a road can lead to less useable fresh water. A major source of the water we use every day is groundwater. Groundwater does not come from lakes or rivers. It comes from underground. The more roads and parking lots we pave, the less water can flow into the ground to become groundwater.
>
> **B.** Human activity is not responsible for all water shortages. Drier climates are of course more likely to have droughts than areas with more rainfall, but regardless of the cause of water shortages, good management can help to make sure there is enough water to meet our basic needs.
>
> **C.** Thinking about the way we use water every day can make a big difference, too. In the United States, a family of four can use 400 gallons of water a day! This shows how much we depend on water to live, but there's a lot we can do to lower that number.
>
> **D.** You can take steps to conserve water in your home. To start with, use the same glass for your drinking water all day. Wash it only once a day. Run your dishwasher only when it is full. Help your parents fix any leaks in your home. That dripping faucet may not seem like much of a problem, but those drops can add up to a lot of wasted water over time! You can even help to keep our water supply clean by recycling batteries instead of throwing them away.

(1) What is this passage mostly about? Check the correct answer below.   10 points

(   ) ⓐ   How droughts occur more in dry climates

(   ) ⓑ   How human activity affects our water supply

(   ) ⓒ   Why paving roads takes away our water

(2) Match each title with the letter of the paragraph it best fits.   30 points for completion

① 400 Gallons a Day   (   )

② Paving Our Way Dry   (   )

③ Enough for Everybody   (   )

(3) Look at the chart of details for paragraph **D**. Then choose a title for the paragraph from the box below.   10 points

Title:
Reuse your drinking glass before washing Run the dishwasher only when full Fix leaks

Possible titles:

Ways to Conserve Water at Home Keeping Water Clean at Home Not Enough Water at Home Sharing Water With Your Family

Water conservation is important!

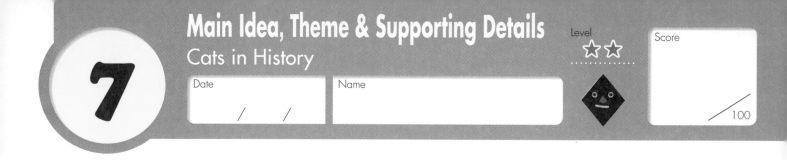

Main Idea, Theme & Supporting Details
Cats in History

7

Level ☆☆

Date / /

Name

Score /100

1 Read the passage. Then answer the questions below.

A. The cat that curls up in your living room chair is distantly related to the mighty lion that is known as the king of its grassland terrain, but the house cat holds its own title. It is the most popular pet in the world. A dog may be man's best friend, but cats live in more homes than any other animal. There are over 600 million cats living as pets throughout the world. Cats live in one third of American homes. That's a lot of cats!

B. While the number of lions and other big cats is sadly diminishing, house cats continue to thrive alongside humans. In fact, cats have been living with humans for a long time. People may have kept cats as pets for as far back as 10,000 years ago. When people traveled or moved to new places, they brought cats with them. That is one reason why cats can be found in different places. Depending on the society, cats were treated with admiration and respect and sometimes even fear. Cats can be seen in ancient Egyptian paintings. The ancient Egyptians used cats to scare away rodents and pests from their grain.

C. Today, humans still rely on cats to scare away pests. Though they may not need to hunt to survive, cats are very capable hunters. Cats have sharp claws that can be used for gripping, climbing, and tearing. They also have excellent night vision. Cats even utilize their whiskers to tell direction at night. A cat's whiskers can sense tiny changes in the breeze, which helps the cat find its way around and also to hunt!

(1) What would be a good title for the entire passage? Check the best title below.   20 points

   (   ) ⓐ   Cats in the Wild

   (   ) ⓑ   The Many Faces of the House Cat

   (   ) ⓒ   Cats and People: A Long History

   (   ) ⓓ   Cats: the Best Pest Control

(2) Which paragraph would the title "King of Pets" best fit?   10 points

   "King of Pets" would be a good title for Paragraph _____.

(3) Look at the chart of details for paragraph **C**. Then compose a title for the paragraph using words from the paragraph.   10 points

Cats are very _____.
Cats can scare away pests. Cats have strong claws that can tear. Cats have excellent night vision. Cats can use their whiskers to hunt.

Read the passage. Then answer the questions below.

The house cat's cousin, the lion, is also a fierce hunter. Lions are a symbol of strength, power, and courage in many places. We often hear that lions are kings of the jungle. In fact, lions live mostly in grassland terrain, where it is easier to spot prey. As with house cats, their excellent night vision helps lions to be effective hunters. Lions also have whiskers that help them sense movements in the air around them. This ability helps a lion to find its prey, even when it is very dark. Of course, a lion's size makes it capable of hunting much larger prey than the house cat can. A male lion can weigh over 400 pounds!

Lions live together in groups called prides. Within a pride, females do most of the hunting. The males defend the pride's territory. The lions work together, which helps them to catch more food. Though the lions in a pride work together to catch food, sometimes they will fight over food at mealtime.

Lions utilize their powerful roar to communicate with other lions. Lions might roar to gather other members of the pride. An adult lion might roar to communicate with a baby lion, or cub. A lion's roar is also used as a tool to scare away intruding lions. It is so powerful that it can be heard five miles away!

The natural habitats of lions in the world are diminishing. Today, most wild lions live in parts of southern Africa, and a smaller group of Asian lions lives in a sanctuary in India. Lions were once found in Africa, India, the Middle East, parts of Europe, and possibly even South America. Today there are far fewer lions than there once were.

Look at the details of each paragraph's chart. Then complete the main idea of the paragraph supported by the details.

Main Idea	Lions are fierce (1)_____.
Supporting Details	Lions use their excellent night vision to hunt prey. Lions use their whiskers to sense movement at night. Lions live in grassland terrain where it is easier to hunt than in the jungle. Lions can be very big, which helps them catch prey.

Main Idea	Lions live and work together in (2)_____.
Supporting Details	Females hunt for the pride. Males defend the pride's territory from intruders. Lions work together to catch food.

Main Idea	Lions use their powerful (3)_____.
Supporting Details	Lions might roar to gather other lions. An adult lion might roar to communicate with a cub. Lions roar to scare away other lions.

I could fight a lion, right?

Main Idea, Theme & Supporting Details
Running From Skill to Sport

Level

Date / /

Name

Score

/100

8

1 Read the passage. Then answer the questions below.

A. A race is a contest of speed between athletes. In a race, athletes compete to see who can achieve a set goal or reach a destination faster. A race between athletes may be a contest between individuals or a team competition, such as a relay race. A race may be a short contest that requires quick bursts of speed. It can even be a longer competition that lasts weeks. Races range from simple contests run on foot to swimming races using Olympic-sized pools. The oldest form of racing is probably running.

B. In fact, running may be the oldest form of athletic competition. It makes sense that running would have been the first sport. Running is something that humans can do naturally and without special equipment. We cannot know for sure where and when running as a sport first occurred, but we do know that competitive running took place in ancient societies. Short competitive races were held in ancient Egypt. The first ancient Greek Olympics had only one event, a running sprint.

C. Running has developed from a necessary skill into a sport used for competition and fun. In ancient times, the human ability to run was a survival skill, first used for activities such as chasing prey. Running was later used for more complicated tasks. It was used for activities such as quickly delivering important messages in battle. Eventually, running became a form of sport, and the fastest runners were admired athletes. This pattern was true for Native Americans. For them, running was a crucial part of life. Very strong runners were first used to communicate over long distances with other groups. Later, running became a sport for many Native Americans, too.

(1) What would be a good title for the passage? Check the best title below.   20 points

(   ) ⓐ Native American Sports

(   ) ⓑ The Future of Running

(   ) ⓒ The Sport of Running

(   ) ⓓ The Oldest Team Sport

(2) Write the letter of the paragraph that fits the main idea below.   10 points

Running was the first sport.   (   )

Don't forget!

The **theme** of a paragraph or passage explains its subject in simple terms, focusing on the main point or central idea.

---

(3) What is the theme of paragraph **C**?   10 points

Running : from skill to _____

2 Read the passage. Then answer the questions below.

20 points per question

A. In more recent times, different running competitions have continued to evolve. Some of these are long-distance races in which runners run for long periods of time. Some racing competitions include running as only one part of a larger competition.

B. The marathon is a popular long-distance race that is typically 26 miles long. The marathon was not run in the ancient Olympics. It is a more recent competition, usually run on roads. However, the term "marathon" does have ancient roots. It comes from the heroic run supposedly completed by the messenger Pheidippides. It was said that he ran from the battlefield at Marathon to his destination at Athens. The 26-mile length of a marathon is based on the distance between Marathon and Athens. Marathon runners must plan to avoid fatigue over the length of the race.

C. A marathon may have many runners, sometimes thousands. Some marathons are run by both amateur runners and world-class athletes. Although a marathon is a competition between runners, many participants are not concerned with the other runners. They may run to see if they can improve upon their previous running times. They may participate just to see if they can complete the marathon distance.

D. Triathlons began as a form of training for runners. They later became competitions on their own. Participants in a triathlon are each required to complete a running, swimming, and bicycling section. The winner of a triathlon is determined by adding together his or her times in each section of the race, plus the time it took the athlete to connect between sections. Triathletes must train very hard to be able to compete in all three sports.

(1) What is the best title for paragraph **A**? Check the best title below.

( ) ⓐ Changes in Running

( ) ⓑ Top Runners

( ) ⓒ Long-Distance Runners

(2) What is the theme of paragraph **B**? Check the best theme below.

( ) ⓐ History

( ) ⓑ Marathons

( ) ⓒ Running on roads

(3) What is the theme of paragraph **D**? Check the best theme below.

( ) ⓐ Swimming and running

( ) ⓑ Training

( ) ⓒ Triathlons

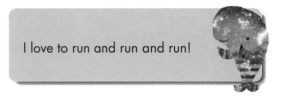

I love to run and run and run!

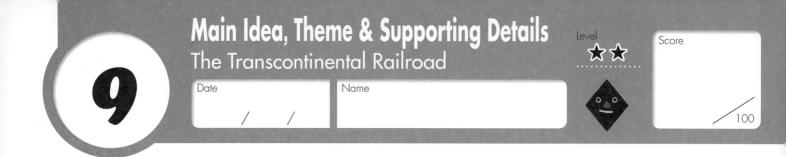

Main Idea, Theme & Supporting Details
The Transcontinental Railroad

9

Level ★★

Score

/100

Date / /

Name

1 Read the passage. Then answer the questions below.

A. The transcontinental railroad changed the United States of America forever. It was a sign of the country's industrial ability, and it was a breakthrough in transportation that made traveling across the country much simpler. It also changed the physical landscape of the country, bringing towns to once-empty land. The railroad brought settlers to different parts of the country and drove many Native Americans from their homes.

B. In the mid-nineteenth century, traveling across the country was much more difficult than it is today. Today, if you wanted to go from New York to California, you could take a plane and arrive in a few short hours. You might even enjoy the view on a cross-country road trip in a car. However, back then, the options were not as convenient. Travelers could sail around the continent by sea, which was expensive. Bold travelers could also go on wagon or foot on routes such as the Oregon Trail. The difficult journey on the Oregon Trail could be dangerous and took as long as six months. The transcontinental railroad was the first convenient option for crossing the United States.

C. The Gold Rush of 1849 helped drive the need for building the transcontinental railroad. Many of those who traveled to California did not find gold, but the rush sparked a boom in California. Towns developed around the miners who depended on local merchants and services. The population of California grew seemingly overnight, driving it toward statehood, but the difficulty of traveling to and from California left the state isolated. By the time of the Civil War, the need for a railroad that would connect the East and West Coasts of the United States was clear.

(1) What would be the best title for paragraph **C**? Check the best title below.   10 points

   ( ) ⓐ How the Civil War Built the Railroad

   ( ) ⓑ The Boom That Brought the Train

   ( ) ⓒ California's Boom

   ( ) ⓓ The Gold Rush

(2) What is the theme of paragraph **B**? Check the best theme below.   10 points

   ( ) ⓐ Taking the plane

   ( ) ⓑ Convenience

   ( ) ⓒ Traveling before the train

(3) What is the main idea of paragraph **A**? Use words from the passage.   20 points

   The _____

   _____ forever.

2 Read the passage. Then answer the questions below.

20 points per question

A. The steam engine was another force behind the building of the transcontinental railroad. Twenty years before the California Gold Rush, people had already dreamed of a railroad that could cross the continent using steam engines. These devices were used to power mills, ships, and eventually trains. The breakthrough of the first steam engine train came in England in 1825. Five years later, the first American steam engine train carried people and goods over a 13-mile track in Maryland.

B. The transcontinental railroad was a display of American industry. Building it took six years and the efforts of two railroad companies. The railroad was built by thousands of determined workers, including many immigrants. These men laid track, built bridges, and blasted through mountain rock at an unbelievable speed. When the last spike was pounded in 1869, travel across the continent was instantly changed. Instead of walking for six months on the Oregon Trail, a person could cross the country in less than a week.

C. The railroad improved communication throughout the country. New and more reliable telegraph wires were set up as it was built. This made it easier for people to send messages to each other. The railroad also greatly increased the speed of mail correspondence.

D. The transcontinental railroad changed where people lived in the country. Boom towns followed the rail workers, often disappearing as the track was laid. However, the railroad's ability to move people and goods in such a short time helped establish permanent settlements far from the continent's coasts. The government encouraged these settlements, often forcing out the Native Americans who already lived on these lands.

The railroad was not to remain the country's only means of convenient transportation, but it had permanently changed America.

(1) What is the theme of paragraph **A**? Check the best theme below.

( ) ⓐ   The California Gold Rush

( ) ⓑ   The railroad dream

( ) ⓒ   The first American steam engine

(2) What is the theme of paragraph **B**? Check the best theme below.

( ) ⓐ   Immigrants working on the railroad

( ) ⓑ   The railroad and American industry

( ) ⓒ   The railroad companies

(3) What is the main idea of the entire passage? Check the best main idea below.

( ) ⓐ   The transcontinental railroad changed America.

( ) ⓑ   The steam engine changed the railroad.

( ) ⓒ   The railroads became faster.

When was the last time you took a ride on a train?

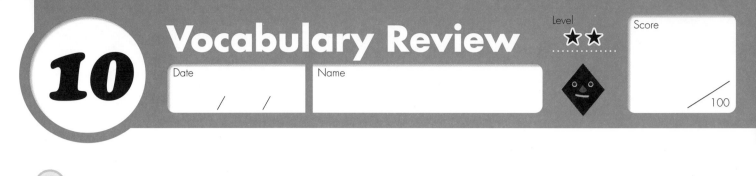

1 Pick the correct word from the box to complete each sentence below.

5 points per question

| merchant | isolated | management | terrain | capable | conserve |

(1) We were worried when the weather changed, but our captain was very _____ and got us through the storm easily.

(2) The _____ of the zoo was questioned when the tiger escaped.

(3) When camping, it's very important to _____ your water.

(4) The _____ proudly displayed his products at the local fair.

(5) Julie was fast when the race was on flat ground, but struggled when the _____ got hilly.

(6) Kevin's aunt lives on an _____ island off the coast of Maine.

2 Read the sentences. Then choose a word from each sentence to match each definition below.

5 points per question

--Nancy Reagan published her famous correspondence with her husband Ronald.

--We finally discovered the source of the smell when we found his old socks.

--Once the disastrous event had occurred, there was no going back.

--The concrete was crucial to our plan, so I went out to get more.

--The library is right on the way to school, so it's very convenient for me.

--The railroads helped establish many towns as they spread to the West.

(1) _____ point of origin

(2) _____ to start or set up something

(3) _____ important or essential

(4) _____ suited to personal comfort; close at hand

(5) _____ letters exchanged

(6) _____ happened

3 Complete the crossword puzzle using the sentences below as clues. Use capital letters.

5 points per question

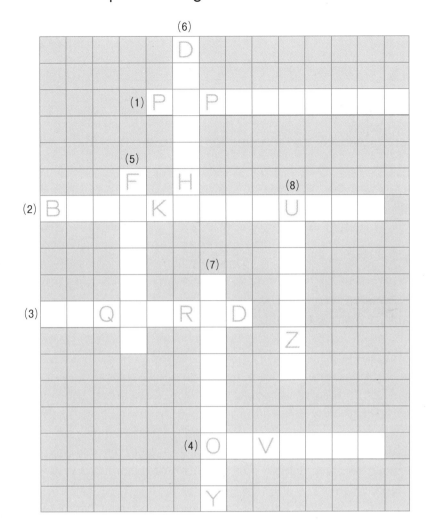

ACROSS

(1) The ___?___ of New York City is over ten million people!

(2) Scientific ___?___ in computing have led to smaller computers.

(3) The teacher let me know that a signed permission slip was ___?___ by today.

(4) What you may think is ___?___ might be harder to understand for others.

DOWN

(5) Marathon runners have to battle ___?___ for much of the race.

(6) The ___?___ has really hurt the crops in our area.

(7) The Lewis family has a dog that insists on defending his ___?___ by barking.

(8) Being good at chess requires finding the best way to ___?___ your pieces.

Way to go!

Interpreting Text
Calvin's New Art

Level ★★

Score
/100

1 Read the passage. Then answer the questions below.

As the due date for his self-portrait neared, Calvin only grew more and more nervous. One by one, his classmates handed in their pictures and sketches to their art teacher, Mrs. Rivera. Some of **them** were black and white sketches, and some were brightly colored paintings. One of his friends turned in a realistic portrait that somehow made his head look three-dimensional. Another student had turned her face into a mosaic, using pieces of tile to make her face look like a puzzle. A third classmate had painted his head using only primary colors. Calvin didn't know why anyone would want to have blue hair, but Mrs. Rivera seemed to like it.

Calvin sat in the back of the class, looking sullen as he eyed the pile of portraits on Mrs. Rivera's desk. However crazy some of his classmates' ideas seemed, he knew that each picture was better than any of his own poor attempts at his portrait. The project was due in a week, and still Calvin had no idea what he would hand in. He always had creative ideas, yet he couldn't seem to draw a straight line. **His** pictures never looked the way he wanted them to when he started.

At the end of class that day, Mrs. Rivera asked Calvin to install some new software on her computer. **This** was not surprising to Calvin. While Calvin may not have been very good at art, everyone knew he was good with computers. Calvin looked at the box for the computer program Mrs. Rivera had given him, which had a picture of a paintbrush over a piece of graph paper. "What's this?" asked Calvin.

"I was hoping you'd ask," said Mrs. Rivera. "It's a computer graphics program that we can use to make pictures."

(1) Identify what the words in bold refer to.

10 points per question

① Some of **them** were black and white sketches.

Some of the classmates' _____ were black and white sketches.

② **His** pictures never looked the way he wanted them to when he started.

_____ pictures never looked the way he wanted them to when he started.

③ **This** was not surprising to Calvin.

That Mrs. Rivera _____

_____ was not surprising to him.

(2) Answer the question below using words from the passage.

10 points

Why was it not surprising to Calvin that Mrs. Rivera asked him for help?

It was not surprising to Calvin that Mrs. Rivera asked him for help because everyone knew that he was _____.

"It's supposed to be for our next unit, which is about graphic design. Everyone in class will have to learn to use this program to make a piece of art. I'm very excited because it's the first time I've ever done this unit with a class. I thought that after you install the program from the disk, you might want to use **it** to create your self-portrait. Then you can teach the class how to use the software."

Calvin liked the thought of being the one to teach his classmates how to do something in art class. **He** learned how to use the program very quickly. The program had tools that the artist could choose from. One corner of the screen showed primary colors that the artist could mix to make new ones. The artist could also draw lines and change the size of the picture. There was even a mosaic option, **which** broke the artist's picture into tiles that could be moved around the screen. Calvin knew that a computer was not going to make him into an artist overnight, but Mrs. Rivera's idea gave him confidence.

Calvin started his portrait by looking in a mirror. **This** was how Mrs. Rivera had told the class they should begin their portraits. He thought about what he looked like and what he wanted to show in his picture. Then he scanned a picture into Mrs. Rivera's computer. The program then allowed him to manipulate the photograph with the artist's tools. When Calvin was finished, he could not believe that he had created his picture without picking up a paintbrush or pencil. Calvin knew that **it** would not look the same on paper as it did on the computer screen, so instead of printing out his picture, he emailed the file to Mrs. Rivera.

(1) He might want to use **it** to create his self-portrait.

He might want to use _____ to create his self-portrait.

(2) **He** learned how to use the program quickly.

_____ learned how to use the program quickly.

(3) ... **which** broke the artist's picture into tiles.

The _____ broke the artist's picture into tiles.

(4) **This** was how Mrs. Rivera had told the class they should start.

_____ was how Mrs. Rivera had told the class they should start.

(5) Calvin knew that **it** would not look the same on paper.

Calvin knew that _____ would not look the same on paper.

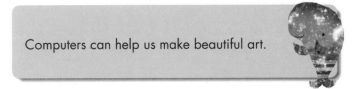

Computers can help us make beautiful art.

23

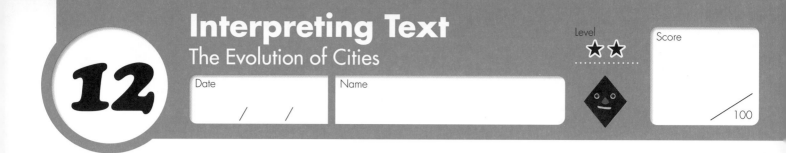

Interpreting Text
The Evolution of Cities

Level ★ ★

Date / /

Name

Score /100

1 Read the passage. Then identify what the words in bold refer to.

10 points per question

> You probably have a clear idea of what makes a city. Maybe you think of a place with crowds, very tall buildings, and loud traffic on hectic streets. The word city may also bring to mind advanced technology and public bus or train systems. A city may have many industries and offices where people go to work. Cities are often cultural and entertainment centers. **This** means that they may have buildings such as theaters, athletic stadiums, and museums. Though cities may seem like a modern idea, some form of them has existed for a long time.
>
> At one time, many cities in Europe and the Middle East had walls that defined their limits. However, **they** were also defined by the people who lived in them. Earlier, people needed to find or hunt for their own food. They moved around instead of living in one place. Improvements in farming meant that people could stay in one place and live in settlements. Some people even developed specialized skills, becoming the craftsmen and merchants who were important to city life.
>
> Another thing that led to the growth of cities was the spread of the wheel. The wheel improved transportation. **This** meant that food and other goods could be transported more easily into cities from other places. People in cities could survive without growing, farming, or catching their own food because **they** bought it from those who did!
>
> Cities may be nothing new, but they are certainly much bigger than they were. One hundred years ago, only a few cities had a population that reached or exceeded one million. Today, many metropolises around the world have millions of people living and working in them.

(1) **This** means that they may have buildings such as theaters, stadiums, and museums.

The fact that cities are often _____
means that they may have buildings such as theaters, stadiums, and museums.

(2) However, **they** were also defined by the people who lived in them.

However, _____ were also
defined by the people who lived in them.

(3) **This** meant that food and other goods could be transported more easily into cities.

The fact that the wheel _____ meant that food and
other goods could be transported more easily into cities.

(4) **They** bought food from others who grew, farmed, or caught it for them.

_____ bought food from others who grew, farmed, or caught it for
them.

Read the passage. Then identify what the words in bold refer to.

15 points per question

> About half of the world's people now live in cities, and the numbers are growing. In the next two decades, two thirds of the world's population will live in cities. This growth means that careful city planning is important to the world's future. The handling of the world's resources and how people receive **them** will depend upon how cities are managed.
>
> Many of the most populated cities in the world are in Asia, which has the world's highest population. Africa and South America also have highly populated cities that are expected to grow in the future. It can be difficult to get an accurate count of the number of people who live in a city. This is because the limits of a city are not always clear. However, two of the largest cities in the world are surely Mumbai, India, and Shanghai, China. **Both** have populations that far exceed 10 million people.
>
> Suburban areas that surround cities are sometimes included in a city's population count. Improvements in transportation not only let goods be transported into a city, **they** have also allowed people to live outside the city, commute into it, and travel around it. In many places, suburbs are often the wealthy and less hectic areas outside of their city centers. People in the suburbs may live in houses, and they may enjoy more space than people inside the city. In other places, suburbs, although less hectic places, are very poor areas compared to the nearby wealthy cities.
>
> In the United States, many people live in city suburbs. **This** is in part a result of the invention of the automobile, which has had a large effect on how people throughout the country live and work. Metropolises such as New York City, Chicago, and Los Angeles have large suburban areas.

(1) How people receive **them** will depend upon how cities are managed.

How people receive _____ will depend on how cities are managed.

(2) **Both** have populations that far exceed 10 million people.

_____ have populations that far exceed 10 million people.

(3) **They** have also allowed people to live outside the city, commute into it, and travel around it.

_____ have also allowed people to live outside the city, commute into it, and travel around it.

(4) **This** is in part a result of the invention of the automobile.

The fact that many _____ is in part a result of the invention of the automobile.

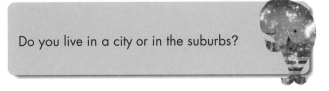

Do you live in a city or in the suburbs?

Interpreting Text
Nomads Around the World 1

13

Level ★★

Date / /

Name

Score /100

1 Read the following passage. Then complete the passage using the vocabulary words defined below.

5 points per question

> Nomads move from one place to another to make a living, usually in groups called (1)_____. The (2)_____ of the nomad includes traveling to find new pastures for livestock and carrying goods to markets. The area that nomads travel through can (3)_____ great distances or be limited to small territories.
>
> Settled peoples are often (4)_____ toward nomads because they fear or do not understand nomadic societies' (5)_____ or values. As a result, many nomads have been (6)_____ from the areas in which they traditionally traveled.
>
> Nomads often live in (7)_____ environments like the Bedouin in the desert and the Inuit in the Arctic. Regardless of where they live, nomads also enjoy a (8)_____ of meat from local animals as well as local fruits and vegetables.

lifestyle	the way someone lives
uproot(ed)	to be moved from one's home or familiar area
culture	a society's ideas, values, customs, and art
tribe(s)	a group sharing the same customs, religion and language
span	to stretch over a distance or period of time
diet	the food a person usually eats
bleak	barren or exposed
hostile	unfriendly; aggressive

2 Read the passage. Then complete the **interpretation** of the **bold** words using other words from the passage.

20 points

> Nomads are either hunters or gatherers, "pastoral" or herding nomads, or craft-workers and merchants. Although traveling has been a way of life for all of these groups, the nomadic lifestlyle is in decline. Some people **point the finger at governments** that are hostile to nomads for this decline, particularly blaming those responsible for uprooting nomadic groups from areas in which they traditionally traveled.

Interpretation: To **point the finger at governments** means _____ these governments

for _____ nomadic groups.

3 Read the passage. Then complete the **interpretation** of the **bold** words using other words from the passage.

10 points per question

> Attempts by scholars to find **a common denominator** amongst different nomad cultures, such as the Bedouin and North American Plains tribes, have largely been abandoned. There are only a few similar cultural elements found amongst nomads that continue to travel through parts of Africa, Asia, Australia, South America, and the far north of Canada, Greenland, Russia, and Alaska.

(1) Interpretation: **A common denominator** refers to something _____ amongst

_____ nomadic groups.

> Many people commonly known as "Gypsies" prefer to be called "Roma." Most Roma speak variations of Romany, a language that originated in northern India. Because Roma typically migrate along routes that ignore national boundaries, the ability to speak more than one language is **not unheard of**. It is not unusual for Roma to speak Romany and the language of the countries in which they travel.

(2) Interpretation: **Not unheard of** refers to the claim that _____ for Roma to speak more than one language.

> The Roma did not leave India as one group; different Roma groups traveled in **successive migrations**. They were in Persia by the eleventh century, southeastern Europe by the fourteenth, and western Europe by the fifteenth. Through continuous migrations, Roma groups had spread to every inhabited continent by the twentieth century.

(3) Interpretation: **Successive migrations** refers to the claim that more than one _____ of

Roma had _____ from India through _____ migrations.

> Nomadic groups have been **plying various trades** all over the world for centuries. They have been traveling entertainers, merchants and craftspeople. Some have been experts on livestock, helping local farmers they have met on their travels. While some nomads can still be found working in these occupations today, many have settled permanently.

(4) Interpretation: "**To ply**" means "to work."

Plying various trades refers to _____

in different _____.

Time to move on!

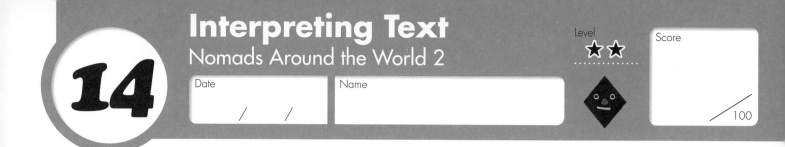

Interpreting Text
Nomads Around the World 2

14

Level ★★

Date / /

Name

Score /100

1 Read each passage. Then complete the interpretation of the underlined part using words from the passage. (**Do not** use the underlined words in your answer.) 10 points per question

> The normally nomadic people of the Arctic region are called the Inuit. In their bleak, often hostile environment with very little vegetation, <u>the Inuit's staple diet has traditionally been Arctic-dwelling animals.</u> Although rifles have largely replaced the harpoons, spears, bows and arrows the Inuit once used for hunting, seals, caribou, and other animals that live in the Arctic continue to be a main food source.

(1) Animals that live in the Arctic have traditionally been a _____ for the Inuit.

> <u>Caribou was the primary source of provisions for many Inuit groups.</u> Hunting caribou provided food, clothing, shelter, and other basic supplies. The Inuit ate caribou meat and used the skins of these reindeer to make the tents that they sheltered in during the summer and the clothing that helped them withstand the cold arctic climate in the winter.

(2) Caribou, a type of _____, was the source of basic _____ for many Inuit groups.

> In the summer, the Inuit traditionally live in tents. <u>Igloos, the home most associated with the Inuit, are interim dwellings over the coldest months of the year used by Inuit in Canada and Greenland.</u> Typically used as short-term, hunting-ground homes during the winter, igloos are furnished with a shallow saucer to burn seal blubber for heat and light.

(3) Igloos are _____ dwellings used during _____ by Inuit living in Canada and Greenland.

> To build an igloo, <u>a sword-like utensil, or "snowknife," is used to meticulously extract blocks of snow from deep snowdrifts.</u> After the first layer of compact snow has been carefully cut out, the tops of the blocks are shaved to form an angle. It is extremely important that the blocks of snow are not damaged, as this would weaken the finished igloo.

(4) A sword-like utensil, or "snowknife," is used to carefully _____ blocks of _____ snow from deep snowdrifts.

2 Read each passage. Then complete the interpretation of the underlined part using words from the passage. (**Do not** use the underlined words in your answer.) 20 points per question

> The Inuktitut language is spoken widely by Inuit living in Canada and Greenland. <u>Though the written language sometimes uses Roman letters, a syllabic script has gained popular acceptance.</u> Inuktitut writing, which is based on sounds unique to the language, owes much of its origins to English missionaries John Horden, E. A. Watkins and Edmund Peck.

(1) Though the written language sometimes uses Roman letters, a system of _____ is widely accepted among the Inuit.

> <u>The Inuktitut language forms a linguistic chain that spans the entire width of northernmost North America.</u> People who study languages treat the regional varieties — from the Alaskan dialects to the eastern Inuktitut languages of Canada — as a single language group because, even though people who live far apart cannot understand each other, each dialect can be understood between people in neighboring regions.

(2) The Inuktitut language is a _____ which is spread across northernmost North America.

3 Read the passage. Then answer the question using words from the passage. (**Do not** use the underlined words in your answer.) 20 points

> There are many traditional Inuit games, including juggling, tug-o-war, and blanket tossing (a trampoline-like game played with a blanket of seal or walrus skin that can withstand heavy pounding).
> <u>Tug-o-war games take on various forms; some are used more as social activities than competitions.</u> One version uses two attached pieces of bone. A man and a woman each hold one bone in their teeth and try to make each other fall. The goal is for the two to become acquainted, not to demonstrate who is the stronger of the two.
> Foreign influences can be found in some Inuit games. *Biblioquet*, a game that utilizes a ball attached to a stick, is also played in Japan, Mexico, and Italy.

What is meant by the underlined part of the text which describes some tug-o-war games as being more social activities than competitions?

Some tug-o-war games are more social activities than competitions because they help men and

women _____ and are not played _____

_____ .

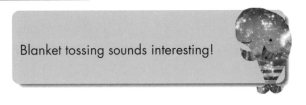

Blanket tossing sounds interesting!

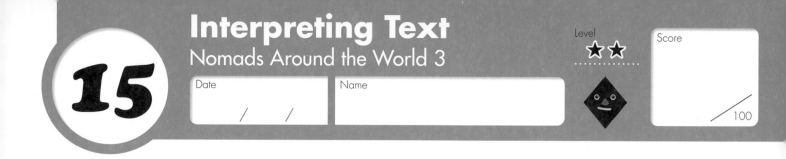

Interpreting Text
Nomads Around the World 3

15

Level ★★

Date / /

Name

Score /100

1 Read each passage. Then answer the questions below.

25 points per question

> *Inupiat, Yupik, Alutiit,* and *Inuit* are variations of the same name for native peoples of the Arctic region. These names mean "the people," or "the real people." Today there are about 150,000 Inuit of various groups living in Greenland, Alaska, Canada, and Siberia. Totally adapted to life on the bleak Arctic terrain, the Inuit have taken advantage of available resources to secure such necessities as food, shelter, and clothing for centuries.
>
> Numerous altercations with societies living to the south of the Inuit homelands have dramatically affected the traditional Inuit way of life, particularly in the twentieth century. Colonialists' powerful, and sometimes hostile, influences have forced many Inuit to abandon their nomadic hunting lifestyle and traditional utensils.

(1) In what way has hostility between the Inuit and societies living to the south affected the traditional Inuit way of life? Use words from the passage.

Hostility between the Inuit and societies living to the south has affected the traditional Inuit way

of life by forcing many _____

_____.

> The Mongols live in the vast plateau of Central Asia. They are a tribal people who share a common language and lifestyle. Mongolian nomads were once divided into clans, and these clans gradually merged into tribes. Some tribal leaders became very powerful, like Genghis Khan in the thirteenth century. Under the leadership of Genghis Khan, the Mongols created one of the world's largest empires.
>
> The Mongols traditionally resided in tents known as *yurts*. While some Mongolians in suburban and rural areas still live in *yurts*, their use has slowly declined. Mongolia's largest city, Ulaanbaatar, once consisted of clusters of *yurts*. By the late twentieth century, *yurts* had become a diminished feature of the city, only found in peripheral regions.

(2) By the late twentieth century, what had happened to the clusters of *yurts* that were once part of the city of Ulaanbaatar?

By the late twentieth century, the use of *yurts* had _____ in the city of Ulaanbaatar,

and they had become a _____ of the city.

2 Read each passage. Then answer the questions below.

The Bedouin are an Arabic-speaking people of the Middle Eastern deserts, concentrated mainly in Saudi Arabia, Iraq, Syria, and Jordan. Though the Bedouin are a small part of the population of the Middle East, they utilize large areas of land over the course of a year.

The Bedouin are pastoral nomads. Every year they move their livestock into the desert in the winter, and back to pastureland in the summer. Some Bedouin herd camels, while others herd goats or cattle.

<u>Although the Bedouin traditionally disliked agricultural work, many of them have become sedentary due to political developments.</u> Following World War I, Bedouin lands were split amongst several nations, which forced many Bedouin to give up their nomadic lifestyle and settle permanently.

(1) What does the underlined part of the passage mean? (Use words from the passage. **Do not** use the underlined words in your answer.)

Although the Bedouin traditionally disliked agricultural work, many of them have been forced to

give _____ because their _____

_____ amongst several nations.

Unlike nomads in other parts of the world, South American forest dwellers rarely herd animals. These nomads prefer hunting, fishing, gathering, and farming instead.

Before occupation of South America by the Spanish and Portuguese, nomads could be found from the southernmost tip of South America to the Orinoco River in the north. Two examples are the Guayak, who utilized the forests of eastern Paraguay to hunt jaguars and armadillos, and the Guat of the upper Paraguay River, whose diet consisted largely of fish.

<u>The seizure of South America and subjugation* of its native peoples by European colonialists slowly uprooted many forest-dwelling tribes.</u> Years of oppression have threatened both their nomadic lifestyle and cultural heritage.

*subjugation - loss of independence or power to another force

(2) Which of the following statements is the best interpretation of the underlined text? Put a check by the correct answer.

( ) ⓐ The occupation of South America by European colonialists uprooted Spanish and Portuguese forest-dwelling peoples.

( ) ⓑ The occupation of South America and oppression by the Spanish and Portuguese slowly uprooted forest-dwelling peoples.

( ) ⓒ South America was occupied by European colonialists, who uprooted many forest-dwelling peoples but not native peoples.

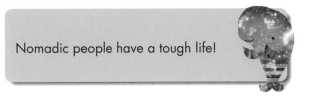

Nomadic people have a tough life!

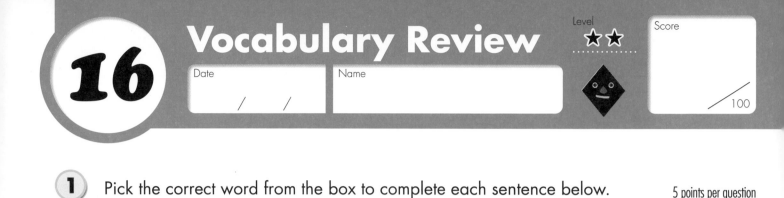

Vocabulary Review

Level ★★

Date / /

Name

Score /100

1 Pick the correct word from the box to complete each sentence below.

5 points per question

| merged | seize | linguistics | utensil | hostile | migrate |

(1) Lee's family has many books because his mother is a professor of _____.

(2) Sometimes the neighbor's dog is _____ towards me.

(3) The two paths _____ in the forest.

(4) In the winter, ducks often _____ south for better weather.

(5) George searched through the kitchen drawer for the correct _____ for the job.

(6) If I ever have the chance to travel the world, I will _____ that opportunity.

2 Read the sentences. Then choose a word from each sentence to match each definition below.

5 points per question

--He noticed the ball coming towards him in his peripheral vision.

--Three days into the camping trip, Javier's provisions were running low.

--Lindsey's cousin is a nomad of sorts, as he's always traveling around the world.

--Since the trip was short, Lolo only took her necessities and packed light.

--New York City is the most famous metropolis in America.

--The ancient people of New Mexico lived in dwellings built right into the sides of cliffs.

(1) _____ needed materials and supplies

(2) _____ major or capital city of a country, state, or region

(3) _____ describing the outer part of something

(4) _____ shelters or houses

(5) _____ things that are needed

(6) _____ a member of a wandering group of people

3 Complete the crossword puzzle using the sentences below as clues. Use capital letters.

5 points per question

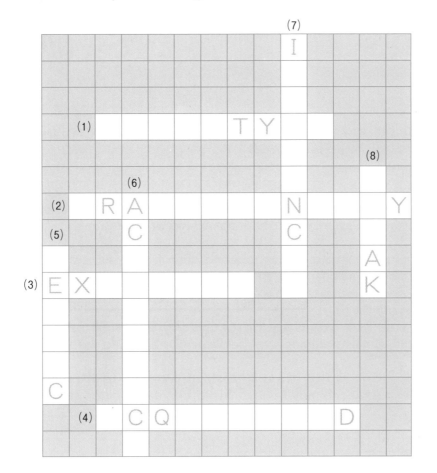

ACROSS

(1) The ___?___ of a professional athlete is not as glamorous as it might seem.

(2) ___?___, the head of the family cuts the roast at our holiday dinner.

(3) Once the number of people in line ___?___ the number of people that could fit in the theater, some people were sent home.

(4) "I am glad to have become ___?___ with you," said my new friend as she left.

DOWN

(5) Our bookstore is always very ___?___ because of the last-minute shoppers before the holidays.

(6) As we do more and more with our computers every day, digital art has also recently gained ___?___.

(7) Gravity is a force that ___?___ the behavior of objects on earth.

(8) The Arctic tundra is a very ___?___ place with few trees or animals.

You got it.

Fact & Opinion

Date   /   /

Name

Level ★★

Score   /100

---

1 Read the explanation and then decide if the following sentences are facts or opinions. Write "**F**" or "**O**" in the space provided.

4 points per question

> ### Don't forget!
>
> A **fact** is something either known to be true or which can be proven to be true.
> An **opinion** is what someone thinks about something or someone.
>
> An opinion will not be shared by all people and often will be subject to disagreement. Even though a person may believe strongly that his or her opinion is true, unless it is provable, it still is an opinon.
>
> Example: Fact: **This hall has a seating capacity of ten thousand.**
> The truth of this statement can be shown by counting the seats.
>
> Opinion: **She is the most beautiful woman in the world.**
> Although someone may believe this to be true, another person might not agree.

(1)   Switzerland has the most picturesque scenery of any country in Europe.   (   )

(2)   The first President of the United States was George Washington.   (   )

(3)   Last night's performance of *Hamlet* was superb.   (   )

(4)   Beijing is the capital of the People's Republic of China.   (   )

---

2 Read the passage and then complete the statement below.

18 points

> The giant panda is a native inhabitant of southwestern China and eastern Tibet, and it feeds mainly on the bamboo that grows in the forests of this region. The black patches circling the eyes on a white face give the giant panda a sad appearance.

Fact: The giant panda lives in the _____ of southwestern China and eastern

_____ and feeds upon the _____ that grows there.

3 Read each passage. Then complete each fact or opinion statement below. <u>18 points per question</u>

> The Metropolitan Museum of Art, sometimes known as "the Met," is the largest art museum in the United States. It contains about 20 acres of floor space at its main location on Fifth Avenue in New York City. Go there to see one of the finest displays of Egyptian art, including a tomb dated about 2460 B.C., or go to a special branch of the Museum called "The Cloisters," which is devoted to medieval art. "The Cloisters" is located in Fort Tyron Park and features some of the most lovely outdoor gardens in New York.

（1） Opinion: _____ has some of the most _____ gardens in New York.

> The Japanese cars on display at the motor show exhibit many innovations and represent the shape of things to come in the auto world. The American cars on display will be released for sale before the end of June. None of the other manufacturers, however, have announced when their cars will be released onto the domestic market.

（2） Fact: The other car _____

have not yet announced when they will

release their _____ onto the

_____ market.

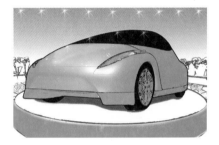

4 Decide whether each of the following sentences is a fact or an opinion. Write "**F**" or "**O**" in the space provided. <u>6 points per question</u>

（1） The sum of the angles in any triangle is 180 degrees. （　　）

（2） New York is the most exciting city in the world. （　　）

（3） The weather was terrible yesterday. （　　）

（4） Harley-Davidson motorbikes are the best on the road. （　　）

（5） The fastest land mammal is the cheetah. （　　）

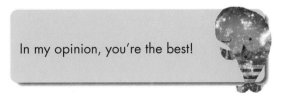

In my opinion, you're the best!

18 Fact & Opinion

Date   /   /   Name

1 Read each passage. Then complete each fact or opinion statement below.   15 points per question

> The first woman in space was the Soviet cosmonaut Valentina Tereshkova. She was working on the assembly line of a textile factory when she was chosen by Premier Nikita Khrushchev to enter the space program. On June 16, 1963, she was launched into space. She piloted the Vostok 6 for three days as it orbited the Earth.

(1) Fact: The _____ was piloted by the Soviet _____ Valentina Tereshkova

for three days, making her the first _____ in space.

> The Spanish artist Pablo Picasso was one of the most creative artists of the twentieth century. He began painting as a young child, experimenting with many styles and subjects. In 1937, during the midst of the Spanish Civil War, he painted *Guernica*, a terrifying vision of destruction and the greatest protest against war by an artist.

(2) Opinion: Pablo Picasso's _____ represents the greatest _____ by an

_____ against war.

2 Decide whether each of the following sentences is a fact or an opinion. Write "**F**" or "**O**" in the space provided.   4 points per question

(1) The Nile and the Amazon are the two longest rivers in the world.   (   )

(2) One mile is approximately 5,280 feet.   (   )

(3) Open-heart surgery is the most difficult operation for doctors.   (   )

(4) Space exploration is humankind's greatest adventure.   (   )

(5) There are 206 bones in an adult human body compared to 300 in a child.   (   )

3 Read each passage. Then complete the fact or opinion statements below. 15 points per question

> The crayfish lives in fresh water and is related to the lobster. The crayfish has five pairs of legs. The front pair serve as claws for catching prey and the other four pairs are used for walking. Europeans regard the crayfish as a delicacy.

(1) Fact: The crayfish uses its _____ pair of legs to grasp its _____ and the

remaining _____ pairs of legs to move about.

> The Dead Sea is situated between Israel and Jordan, with a section of it representing the border between the two countries. The beautiful surroundings of colored mountains, the sparkling water, and the excellent buoyancy make the Dead Sea a relaxing place to swim.

(2) Opinion: The Dead Sea is a _____ place for swimming

due to its surroundings, its _____

and excellent _____.

4 Complete the sentences using one of the phrases in each pair of brackets. Choose the correct phrase in order to make the sentence a fact or an opinion as indicated.

5 points per question

(1) Fact:
South Korea is a country _____.

[whose people are kind / bordered by North Korea]

(2) Fact:
The Berlin Wall _____.

[was torn down in 1989 / was the greatest symbol of the cold war]

(3) Opinion:
Baseball caps _____.

[shade the head / are not fashionable]

(4) Opinion:
The White House _____.

[has 132 rooms / is huge and interesting]

You know your facts and opinions!

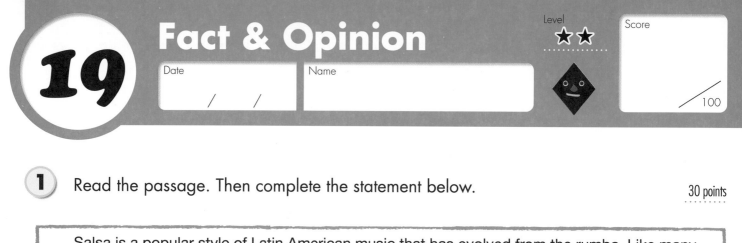

19 Fact & Opinion

Level ★★

Score
/100

Date / /

Name

1 Read the passage. Then complete the statement below.

30 points

> Salsa is a popular style of Latin American music that has evolved from the rumba. Like many other types of Latin American music, salsa and the rumba are both musical and dance styles. Latin America is the region that consists of Central and South America and the Caribbean. Some of the many interesting forms of music produced there include: the samba from Brazil, merengue from the Dominican Republic and Haiti, the tango from Argentina, and reggae from Jamaica. These styles of music and dance have developed from a combination of popular folk traditions and outside influences.

Fact: _____ musical styles such as the tango from Argentina and

the _____ from Brazil are associated with _____ of the same name.

2 Complete the sentences using one of the phrases in each pair of brackets. Choose the correct phrase in order to make the sentence a fact or an opinion as indicated.

5 points per question

(1) Fact:
Golf is a sport that _____.

[is extremely boring / uses long metal clubs to hit a small white ball]

(2) Opinion:
Skyscrapers in major modern cities _____.

[house many businesses / are marvels of engineering]

(3) Fact:
The giraffe is _____.

[the world's most majestic animal / the world's tallest animal]

(4) Opinion:
Notre Dame is the name of _____.

[a cathedral in Paris / the most famous structure in France]

3 Read the passage. Then do the exercises below. 10 points per question

> Big, bulky telephone and television cables are quickly becoming a thing of the past. They are being replaced by bundles of hair-thin glass fiber cables that carry thousands of data circuits per fiber. This technology is called fiber optics. Fiber optics uses laser technology to channel light rays through extremely pure glass rods. Lasers produce intense, highly concentrated beams of single wavelength light. Fiber-optic cables conduct these beams through a minimum-resistance medium of pure glass. The light is prevented from escaping the fiber by total reflection.

(1) What is the main idea of this paragraph? Check the best main idea below.

( )ⓐ This new technology uses lasers that produce weak, dispersed light of many wavelengths.

( )ⓑ This new technology uses lasers that create concentrated beams of light of a single wavelength.

( )ⓒ This new technology uses lasers that are bundles of hair-thin glass fiber cables.

(2) What is the name of the new technology discussed in the passage above?

( )

4 Read the passage. Then complete the statement and the summary below. 15 points per question

> The advantages of fiber optics over older technologies include cable sizes that are much smaller, a much lower cost of materials, immunity from interference, and a vastly increased carrying capacity. Optical fibers can transmit audio, video, and data information as coded light impulses. One example is AT&T's Northeast Corridor Network, with cables running from Virginia to Massachusetts. These cables carry 1,340 voice circuits per fiber pair. Applications currently being developed include power transmission for robotics and intense light and power sources for use in dental and surgical procedures and in car and airplane systems. By placing fibers into bundles, optic plates have revolutionized fax machines and computer graphics.

(1) Fact: Fiber optic _____ running from Virginia to _____

can carry 1,340 voice _____ per fiber pair.

(2) Summary: The author believes that fiber optics can be used to transmit intense _____

and power which can be used for medical and dental operations. Fiber-optic plates

made from _____ of fibers can vastly improve _____ machines

and computer graphics.

Our computers communicate through glass with light!

39

1 Read the passage. Then answer the questions below.

20 points per question

Keeping an animal as a pet may seem like a natural thing in most Western cultures. On the other hand, many people from other cultures may find Western practices strange or immoral. For example, many people in countries around the world believe that dogs are dirty and should not be kept as pets. In some cultures, dogs are considered nuisances that should not be allowed in the house. You may have heard of people keeping pigs as pets, but that also is not allowed by other religions and cultures that see pigs as lazy and unclean.

The cat has had many ups and downs over the history of the world. In ancient Egypt they were deified — there were cat gods! The cat god Bastet was a god that protected fertility, children, and all cats. In Bastet's temple, cats were served, cared for, and even mummified so that they would pass into the afterlife. In Medieval Europe, cats were considered supernatural and were linked to black magic. When the Bubonic Plague erupted in the 14th century, some communities blamed cats and chased them from their towns. Unfortunately, the cats were less at fault than the rodents they hunted, which carried the plague across Europe.

There are also pets in other countries that may seem strange to Western cultures. Hyenas are dangerous animals that can go toe-to-toe with lions, but there are least some groups of people in Syria that keep hyenas as pets. Although tarantulas have venom strong enough to kill small animals, they are also kept as pets around the world.

(1) What is the author's opinion concerning how pets are viewed by people in different cultures? Check the correct answer.

( ) ⓐ People who keep dogs as pets are strange or immoral.

( ) ⓑ People from one culture may find the pets kept by another culture as strange or immoral.

( ) ⓒ People in Western cultures like to keep strange pets.

(2) What was a common opinion about cats in Medieval Europe?

A common opinion about cats in Medieval Europe was that they were considered _____

_____.

2 Read the passage. Then answer the questions below.

20 points per question

Many plants and animals have chemical weapons in the form of poisons or toxins that they use to defend, attack, or exploit the environments in which they live. These natural poisons are complex chemicals that have developed over thousands of years in response to patterns of animal behavior. Toxicology, or the study of poisons, is an important science that studies not only the dangers of posions, but more significantly, how poisons can be used in medicine for the benefit of humankind.

Poisons either occur naturally or are produced by plants and animals from raw materials in the soil or in their foods. For example, cyanide is a simple compound found in millipedes and peach pits. The monarch butterfly, however, makes a poison from the milkweed plant it eats. Poisons can range from being mildly irritating to causing death. They can cause skin irritation, vomiting, or they can poison the blood or nerves. They can also interfere with the functioning of the body by attacking organs such as the heart or lungs. They can interfere with critical life processes, such as molting in insects or photosynthesis in plants.

Many people are scared by rattlesnakes or stingrays because their venom can cause death. These creatures use poison as a response to certain situations that they perceive as dangerous. They have developed poisons in their bodies over a period of centuries. These poisons have allowed them to survive where other species have died.

The benefits of poisons and toxins far outweigh their harmful effects on humankind. Quinine from the bark of the cinchona tree is used to treat malaria, and the science of genetic engineering is greatly enhanced by using modified toxic compounds.

(1) What is the author's opinion concerning people's reactions to rattlesnakes and stingrays? Check the correct answer.

(   ) ⓐ   Many people are scared when they see a rattlesnake biting a stingray.

(   ) ⓑ   Many people are scared by rattlesnakes or stingrays because they have nasty personalities.

(   ) ⓒ   Many people are scared of rattlesnakes or stingrays because of their deadly venom.

(2) What facts concerning cyanide are presented in the article?

Cyanide is a _____

_____ .

(3) Complete the summary.

The study of poisons, called _____ , is not only concerned with the dangers of

poisons and toxins, but also the _____ to humankind. For example, toxicology has

led to the discovery that _____ can be used to treat malaria.

Toxins are scary but helpful too.

1 Pick the correct word from the box to complete each sentence below.

5 points per question

| circuits | concentrated | situated | buoyant | picturesque | approximately |

(1) My room is _____ fifteen feet wide in the middle.

(2) Once the raft is inflated, it will be _____ enough to hold you.

(3) When I took my computer to the shop, the technicians said the _____ were broken.

(4) The school is _____ between the park and the library.

(5) Although I _____ very hard, I couldn't understand the book at all.

(6) The scene from the window of my uncle's farm was very _____.

2 Read the sentences. Then choose a word from each sentence to match each definition below.

5 points per question

--Frog legs are a delicacy in some cultures.

--The Sahara is a vast desert that stretches across much of North Africa.

--Much of medieval art was religious because the church had the money to pay artists.

--Surprisingly, some toxins can help humans if they are used correctly.

--Mosquitos can be a real nuisance in the summer.

--Our library is the biggest in our region.

(1) _____ something that is annoying, unpleasant or obnoxious

(2) _____ an indefinite area of the world

(3) _____ poisonous substance(s)

(4) _____ something pleasing to eat that is considered rare

(5) _____ very great in size (enormous)

(6) _____ relating to the Middle Ages

3 Complete the crossword puzzle using the sentences below as clues. Use capital letters.

5 points per question

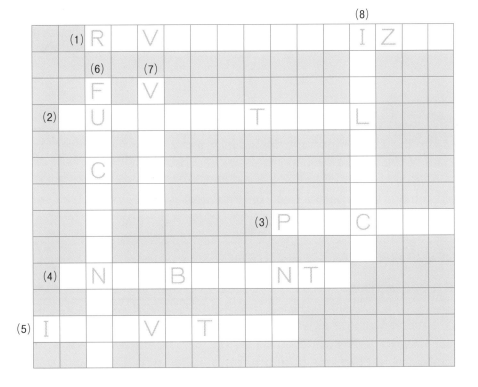

ACROSS

(1) Fiber optic cables have ___?___ computing and the internet.

(2) I don't believe in ___?___ beings, but my brother thinks he sees ghosts.

(3) Cooking is okay. I love to eat, but the ___?___ of making the food takes too long.

(4) The ___?___ of Greenland have to deal with bad weather most days.

(5) High-definition television is a popular ___?___ in the media industry.

DOWN

(6) We have a lot of electronics in the garage, but not one of them is ___?___ right now.

(7) Vipers are deadly because of the ___?___ they inject with their fangs.

(8) Cal's mother always tells him to be a good ___?___ on his brother.

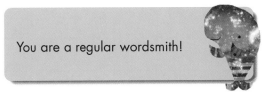

You are a regular wordsmith!

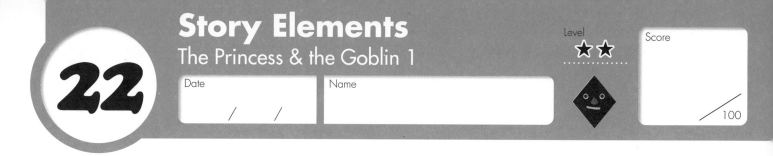

Story Elements
The Princess & the Goblin 1

Level ★★

Date / /

Name

Score /100

22

Don't forget!

Story elements are the most important details in a story. They include *setting, characters, plot,* and *theme.*

1 Read the passage from the opening of *The Princess & the Goblin* by George MacDonald. Then answer the questions below.

12 points per question

WHY THE PRINCESS HAS A STORY ABOUT HER

There was once a little princess whose father was king over a great country full of mountains and valleys. His palace was built upon one of the mountains, and was very grand and beautiful. The princess, whose name was Irene, was born there, but she was sent soon after her birth, because her mother was not very strong, to be brought up by country people in a large house, half castle, half farmhouse, on the side of another mountain, about half-way between its base and its peak.

The princess was a sweet little creature, and at the time my story begins was about eight years old, I think, but she got older very fast. Her face was fair and pretty, with eyes like two bits of the night sky, each with a star dissolved in the blue. Those eyes you would have thought must have known they came from there, so often were they turned up in that direction. The ceiling of her nursery was blue, with stars in it, as like the sky as they could make it. But I doubt if ever she saw the real sky with the stars in it, for a reason which I had better mention at once.

---

(1) Who seems to be the most important person in this story?

The _____ seems to be the most important person in this story.

Don't forget!

The most important character in a story, novel, or play is called the **main character**.

(2) What does the main character look like?

The main character has a face that was _____, with _____

_____, each _____.

(3) Where was the princess brought up?

The princess was brought up in a large _____,

on the side of another _____.

Don't forget!

The time, place, and circumstance in which a story is set is called the **setting**.

2 Read the passage. Then answer the questions below.

16 points per question

These mountains were full of hollow places underneath; huge caverns, and winding ways, some with water running through them, and some shining with all colours of the rainbow when a light was taken in. There would not have been much known about them, had there not been mines there, great deep pits, with long galleries and passages running off from them, which had been dug to get at the ore* of which the mountains were full. In the course of digging, the miners came upon many of these natural caverns. A few of them had far-off openings out on the side of a mountain, or into a ravine*.

Now in these subterranean caverns lived a strange race of beings, called by some gnomes, by some kobolds, by some goblins. There was a legend current in the country that at one time they lived above ground, and were very like other people. But for some reason or other, concerning which there were different legendary theories, the king had laid what they thought too severe taxes upon them, … or had begun to treat them with more severity, in some way or other, and impose stricter laws; and the consequence was that they had all disappeared from the face of the country. According to the legend, however, instead of going to some other country, they had all taken refuge in the subterranean caverns, whence they never came out but at night, and then seldom showed themselves in any numbers, and never to many people at once. It was only in the least frequented and most difficult parts of the mountains that they were said to gather even at night in the open air.

ore - naturally occuring mineral / *ravine* - a narrow steep-sided valley

(1) What is the first paragraph mostly about?

The first paragraph is mostly about the _____ underneath the

mountains and their huge _____ and _____.

> **Don't forget!**
>
> The **theme** of a paragraph explains its subject in simple terms, focusing on the main point or central idea.

(2) What is the theme of the second paragraph?

There was a strange _____ that had taken _____

_____ and never came out but _____.

(3) What was the consequence of all the theories regarding the goblins?

The consequence was that they _____

_____.

(4) Since they had taken refuge in the caverns, when did the goblins come out?

The goblins only came out at _____ and seldom _____

in any numbers, and never _____.

This is setting the scene for a good story!

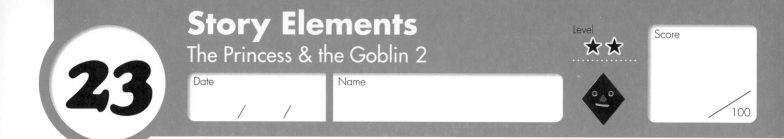

Story Elements
The Princess & the Goblin 2

Level ★★

Score

/100

23

Date / /

Name

1 Read the passage. Then answer the questions below.

Those who had caught sight of any of them said that they had greatly altered in the course of generations; and no wonder, seeing they lived away from the sun, in cold and wet and dark places. They were now, not ordinarily ugly, but either absolutely hideous, or ludicrously* grotesque* both in face and form. There was no invention, they said, of the most lawless imagination expressed by pen or pencil, that could surpass the extravagance of their appearance. But I suspect those who said so had mistaken some of their animal companions for the goblins themselves — of which more by and by. The goblins themselves were not so far removed from the human as such a description would imply. And as they grew misshapen in body they had grown in knowledge and cleverness, and now were able to do things no mortal could see the possibility of. But as they grew in cunning, they grew in mischief and their great delight was in every way they could think of to annoy the people who lived in the open-air storey above them. They had enough of affection left for each other to preserve them from being absolutely cruel for cruelty's sake to those that came in their way; but still they so heartily cherished* the ancestral grudge against those who occupied their former possessions, and especially against the descendants* of the king who had caused their expulsion, that they sought every opportunity of tormenting* them in ways that were as odd as their inventors; and although dwarfed and misshapen, they had strength equal to their cunning.

*ludicrously - describing something done in an amusing, laughable or absurd way / *grotesque - bizarre and ugly
*cherish - to hold dear / *descendant - proceeding from an ancestor / *torment - cause vexation or pain

(1) Fill in the chart below describing the goblins.

8 points per question

Goblin's Characteristics	Descriptions
Face and form	They were absolutely ①_____ or ludicrously grotesque in face and form.
Intelligence	As they grew misshapen in body they had grown in ②_____.
Behavior	As they grew in cunning, they ③_____.

(2) Who did the goblins especially bear a grudge against?

24 points

The goblins still _____ cherished the _____ grudge, especially against the

_____.

Read the passage. Then answer the questions below.

In the process of time, they had got a king and a government of their own, whose chief business, beyond their own simple affairs, was to devise trouble for their neighbours. It will now be pretty evident why the little princess had never seen the sky at night. They were much too afraid of the goblins to let her out of the house then, even in company with ever so many attendants; and they had good reason, as we shall see by and by.

THE PRINCESS LOSES HERSELF

I have said the Princess Irene was about eight years old when my story begins. And this is how it begins.

One very wet day, when the mountain was covered with mist which was constantly gathering itself together into raindrops, and pouring down on the roofs of the great old house, whence it fell in a fringe of water from the eaves* all around about it, the princess could not of course go out. She got very tired, so tired that even her toys could no longer amuse her. You would wonder at that if I had time to describe to you one half of the toys she had. But then, you wouldn't have the toys themselves, and that makes all the difference: you can't get tired of a thing before you have it. It was a picture, though, worth seeing — the princess sitting in the nursery with the sky ceiling over her head, at a great table covered with her toys. If the artist would like to draw this, I should advise him not to meddle with the toys. I am afraid of attempting to describe them, and I think he had better not try to draw them. He had better not. He can do a thousand things I can't, but I don't think he could draw those toys.

*eaves - the lower part of a roof that extends beyond the outer wall

(1) When does the story begin?

The story begins when the Princess Irene was _____.

(2) What is the setting for the beginning of the story?

The setting for the beginning of the story is a very _____, with the mountain

_____.

(3) How was the main character feeling at the beginning of this story?

The main character was very _____, so _____

_____.

(4) When the person telling the story says "He had better not," who is he referring to?

The person telling the story is referring to the _____ who would like to _____ the princess and her toys.

Don't forget!

The person telling the story is called the **narrator**.

You're doing great!

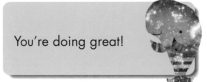

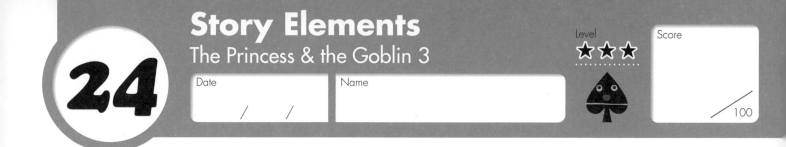

Story Elements
The Princess & the Goblin 3

24

Date / /

Name

Level ★★★

Score /100

1 Read the passage. Then answer the questions below using words from the passage.

10 points per question

No man could better make the princess herself than he could, though — leaning with her back bowed into the back of the chair, her head hanging down, and her hands in her lap, very miserable as she would say herself, not even knowing what she would like, except it were to go out and get thoroughly wet, and catch a particularly nice cold, and have to go to bed and take gruel. The next moment after you see her sitting there, her nurse goes out of the room.

Even that is a change and the princess wakes up a little, and looks about her. Then she tumbles off her chair, and runs out of the door, not the same door the nurse went out of, but one which opened at the foot of a curious old stair of worm-eaten oak, which looked as if never anyone had set foot upon it. She had once before been up six steps, and that was sufficient reason, in such a day, for trying to find out what was at the top of it.

Up and up she ran — such a long way it seemed to her! — until she came to the top of the third flight. There she found the landing was the end of a long passage. Into this she ran. It was full of doors on each side. There were so many that she did not care to open any, but ran on to the end, where she turned into another passage, also full of doors. When she had turned twice more, and still saw doors and only doors about her, she began to get frightened. It was so silent! And all those doors must hide rooms with nobody in them! That was dreadful. Also the rain made a great trampling noise on the roof.

(1) What is the theme of the first paragraph?

The princess is very _____ as she would say herself.

(2) What is the first action by the princess in this story?

The princess wakes up, looks about, _____ off her chair, and _____

_____ .

> **Don't forget!**
> The sequence of actions and events in a story is called the **plot**.

(3) What happened next in the plot?

The princess ran to the top of the _____ of stairs, and then ran into many

passages full of _____ on _____ .

(4) Why did the princess begin to get frightened?

The princess began to get frightened because it was so _____, the doors hid rooms

_____ and the rain made a _____

_____ .

2 Read the passage. Then answer the questions below.

She turned and started at full speed, her little footsteps echoing through the sounds of the rain — back for the stairs and her safe nursery. So she thought, but she had lost herself long ago. ...

She ran for some distance, turned several times, and then began to be afraid. Very soon she was sure that she had lost the way back. Rooms everywhere and no stair! Her little heart beat as fast as her little feet ran, and a lump of tears was growing in her throat. But she was too eager and perhaps too frightened to cry for some time. At last her hope failed her. Nothing but passages and doors everywhere! She threw herself on the floor, and burst into a wailing cry broken by sobs.

She did not cry long, however, for she was ⓐas brave as could be expected of a princess of her age. After a good cry, she got up, and brushed the dust from her frock. Oh, what old dust it was! Then she wiped her eyes with her hands, for princesses don't always have their handkerchiefs in their pockets, ⓑany more than some other little girls I know of. Next, like a true princess, she resolved on going wisely to work to find her way back: she would walk through the passages, and look in every direction for the stair. This she did, but without success. She went over the same ground again and again without knowing it, for the passages and doors were all alike. ⓒAt last, in a corner, through a half-open door, she did see a stair. But alas! it went the wrong way: instead of going down, it went up. Frightened as she was, however, she could not help wishing to see where yet further the stair could lead. It was very narrow, and so steep that she went on like a four-legged creature on her hands and feet.

(1) Why was the main character afraid in the second paragraph?   12 points

The main character was afraid because she was sure _____

_____.

(2) What did the main character do first after realizing she was lost?   12 points

The main character threw _____, and _____

_____ broken by sobs.

(3) Write the letter from each underlined section in the passage that corresponds to each story element listed below.   12 points per question

① The narrator talks about his own life: (   )

② A description of the main character: (   )

③ The next step in the plot: (   )

I hope the princess can find a way out!

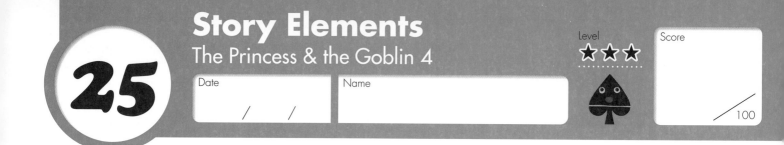

Story Elements
The Princess & the Goblin 4

25

Date / /

Name

Level
★★★

Score
/100

1 Read the passage. Then answer the questions below.

THE PRINCESS AND — WE SHALL SEE WHO

When she came to the top, she found herself in a little square place, with three doors, two opposite each other, and one opposite the top of the stair. She stood for a moment, without an idea in her little head what to do next. But as she stood, she began to hear a curious humming sound. Could it be the rain? No. It was much more gentle, and even monotonous than the sound of the rain, which now she scarcely heard. The low sweet humming sound went on, sometimes stopping for a little while and then beginning again. It was more like the hum of a very happy bee that had found a rich well of honey in some globular flower, than anything else I can think of at this moment. Where could it come from? She laid her ear first to one of the doors to hearken* if it was there — then to another. When she laid her ear against the third door, there could be no doubt where it came from: it must be from something in that room. What could it be? She was rather afraid, but her curiosity was stronger than her fear, and she opened the door very gently and peeped in. What do you think she saw? A very old lady who sat spinning.

Perhaps you will wonder how the princess could tell that the old lady was an old lady, when I inform you that not only was she beautiful, but her skin was smooth and white. I will tell you more. Her hair was combed back from her forehead and face, and hung loose far down and all over her back. That is not much like an old lady — is it? Ah! but it was white almost as snow. And although her face was so smooth, her eyes looked so wise that you could not have helped seeing she must be old.

*hearken - listen

(1) How did the princess know the sound she heard was not the rain?   10 points

The princess knew the sound was not the rain because it was much more _____, and

even more _____ than the sound of rain.

(2) What does the narrator compare the sound to?   10 points

The narrator compares the sound to the hum _____

_____.

(3) Fill in the chart below about the descriptions of the newest character in the story.   10 points per question

Descriptions of the Woman	
Not old-looking	**Old-looking**
Beautiful Skin was ① _____ Hair hung ② _____	Hair was white as snow Eyes looked so ③ _____

2 Read the passage. Then write the letter from each underlined section in the passage that corresponds to each story element listed below.

10 points per question

The princess, though she could not have told you why, did think her very old indeed — quite fifty, she said to herself. But she was rather older than that, as you shall hear.

While (a) the princess stared bewildered, with her head just inside the door, the old lady lifted hers, and said, in a sweet, but old and rather shaky voice, which mingled pleasantly with the continued hum of her wheel: 'Come in, my dear; come in. I am glad to see you.'

That the princess was a real princess you might see now quite plainly; for she didn't hang on to the handle of the door, and stare without moving, (b) as I have known some do who ought to have been princesses but were only rather vulgar* little girls. She did as she was told, (c) stepped inside the door at once, and shut it gently behind her.

'Come to me, my dear,' said the old lady.

And again the princess did as she was told. She approached the old lady — rather slowly, I confess, but did not stop until she stood by her side, and looked up in her face with her blue eyes and the two melted stars in them.

… The little princess wondered to see how straight and tall she was, for, although she was so old, she didn't stoop a bit. (d) She was dressed in black velvet with thick white heavy-looking lace about it; and on the black dress her hair shone like silver. There was hardly any more furniture in the room than there might have been in that of the poorest old woman who made her bread by her spinning. (e) There was no carpet on the floor — no table anywhere — nothing but the spinning-wheel and the chair beside it. …

'Do you know my name, child?'

'No, I don't know it,' answered the princess.

'My name is Irene.'

*vulgar - of or relating to common people

(1) An action that furthers the plot: (   )

(2) A description of the main character: (   )

(3) A description of the new character: (   )

(4) The narrator talks about his own life: (   )

(5) A description of the new setting: (   )

They have the same name! You'll have to find the book,
The Princess & the Goblin by George MacDonald, to know more!

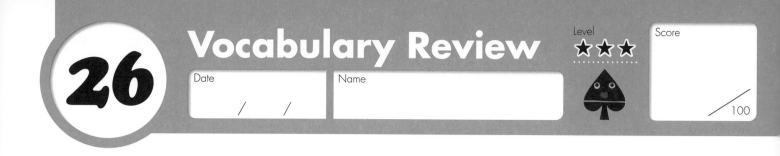

26 Vocabulary Review

Level ★★★

Date / /

Name

Score /100

1 Pick the correct word from the box to complete each sentence below.

5 points per question

| resolved | cherish | wailing | ravine | ore | theme |

(1) The miners carted the _____ back to the surface.

(2) The baby in the seat next to me spent the entire flight _____.

(3) The major _____ of this movie is forgiveness.

(4) After receiving a bad grade on a math test last month, I _____ to study harder.

(5) The hawk made its nest on the side of a steep _____.

(6) My younger cousin promised to _____ the stuffed animal I gave her.

2 Read the sentences. Then choose a word from each sentence to match each definition below.

5 points per question

--The eaves of the roof hung low as they were full of snow.

--My ancestors came from Holland.

--Esperanza's alarm clock makes an annoying, monotonous sound in the mornings.

--The evil baron laughed and told the young thief that it was ludicrous to think he could outsmart the baron.

--After expulsion from the classroom for talking, Rick had to go to the principal's office.

--The subterranean caverns led all the way from the mountains to the sea.

(1) _____ describing something with an unchanging tone or sound

(2) _____ the lower parts of a roof that hang over the edge

(3) _____ underground

(4) _____ amusing or laughable through obvious absurdity

(5) _____ ones from whom a person is descended

(6) _____ the state of being forced out

3 Complete the crossword puzzle using the sentences below as clues. Use capital letters.

5 points per question

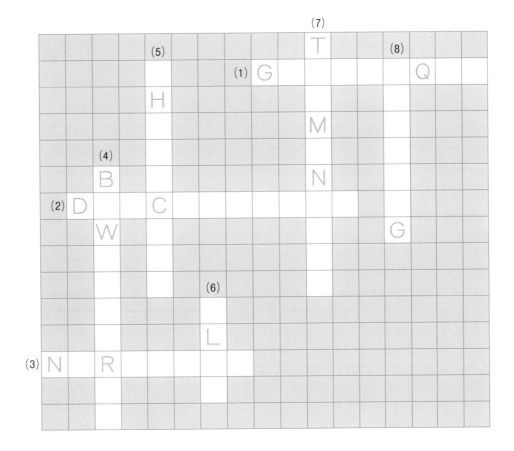

ACROSS

(1) After James' finger got caught in the door, it looked ___?___ and turned all sorts of colors.

(2) Becky is always saying that her father and uncle are ___?___ of Davy Crockett.

(3) I don't like it when the ___?___ of a book makes too many comments about himself.

DOWN

(4) My dad had a ___?___ expression on his face after he got off the spinning ride.

(5) The main ___?___ of my favorite book is a dwarf on a mission.

(6) I liked the book, but Martha didn't think the ___?___ was believable.

(7) Peter's mother told him to stop ___?___ his little brother by teasing him.

(8) The ___?___ for Tina's play was a damp, dark night in a cemetery.

If you need another hint, try going back through the previous pages.

Reading Comprehension
The Lion, the Witch and the Wardrobe 1

27

Level ★★

Date   /   /

Name

Score

/100

1 Read the passage from the opening of *The Lion, the Witch and the Wardrobe* by C.S. Lewis. Then answer the questions below using words from the passage.   10 points per question

> LUCY LOOKS INTO A WARDROBE
>
> Once there were four children whose names were Peter, Susan, Edmund and Lucy. This story is about something that happened to them when they were sent away from London during the war because of the air-raids. They were sent to the house of an old Professor who lived in the heart of the country, ten miles from the nearest railway station and two miles from the nearest post office. He had no wife and he lived in a very large house with a housekeeper called Mrs. Macready and three servants. (Their names were Ivy, Margaret and Betty, but they do not come into the story much.) He himself was a very old man with shaggy white hair which grew over most of his face as well as on his head, and they liked him almost at once; but on the first evening when he came out to meet them at the front door he was so odd-looking that Lucy (who was the youngest) was a little afraid of him, and Edmund (who was the next youngest) wanted to laugh and had to keep on pretending he was blowing his nose to hide it.
>
> As soon as they had said good night to the Professor and gone upstairs on the first night, the boys came into the girls' room and they all talked it over.
>
> "We've fallen on our feet and no mistake," said Peter. "This is going to be perfectly splendid. That old chap will let us do anything we like."
>
> "I think he's an old dear," said Susan.
>
> "Oh, come off it!" said Edmund, who was tired and pretending not to be tired, which always made him bad-tempered. "Don't go on talking like that."
>
> "Like what?" said Susan; "and anyway, it's time you were in bed."
>
> "Trying to talk like Mother," said Edmund. "And who are you to say when I'm to go to bed? Go to bed yourself."

(1) When and why were the children sent away?

The children were sent away during _____.

(2) What did the Professor look like?

The Professor was _____

_____ and head.

(3) Why was Lucy a little afraid of the Professor?

Lucy was a little afraid of the Professor because he was so _____.

(4) Why did Peter think they had fallen on their feet?

Peter thought they had fallen on their feet because the Professor would _____ them _____ they like.

Read the passage. Then answer the questions below using words from the passage.

20 points per question

"Hadn't we all better go to bed?" said Lucy. "There's sure to be a row if we're heard talking here."

"No, there won't," said Peter. "I tell you this is the sort of house where no one's going to mind what we do. Anyway, they won't hear us. It's about ten minutes' walk from here down to that dining room, and any amount of stairs and passages in between."

"What's that noise?" said Lucy suddenly. It was a far larger house than she had ever been in before and the thought of all those long passages and rows of doors leading into empty rooms was beginning to make her feel a little creepy.

"It's only a bird, silly," said Edmund.

"It's an owl," said Peter. "This is going to be a wonderful place for birds. I shall go to bed now. I say, let's go and explore tomorrow. You might find anything in a place like this. Did you see those mountains as we came along? And the woods? There might be eagles. There might be stags*. There'll be hawks."

"Badgers!" said Lucy.

"Foxes!" said Edmund.

"Rabbits!" said Susan.

But when next morning came there was a steady rain falling, so thick that when you looked out of the window you could see neither the mountains nor the woods nor even the stream in the garden.

"Of course it *would* be raining!" said Edmund. They had just finished their breakfast with the Professor and were upstairs in the room he had set apart for them — a long, low room with two windows looking out in one direction and two in another.

*stag - an adult male deer

(1) Why couldn't the staff hear the children talking?

The staff couldn't hear them talking because it was about _____ from

their room down _____, with any _____

_____.

(2) What made Lucy feel creepy?

Lucy felt creepy because she was in a far _____

_____, with all those long _____

_____.

(3) How thick was the rain in the morning?

The rain was so thick that when _____

you could see neither the _____

_____.

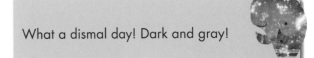

What a dismal day! Dark and gray!

55

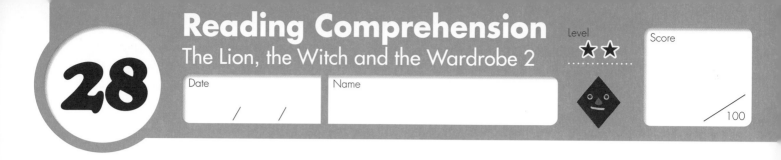

Reading Comprehension
The Lion, the Witch and the Wardrobe 2

Level ★★

Score

/100

Date / /

Name

1 Read the passage. Then answer the questions below.

16 points per question

> "Do stop grumbling, Ed," said Susan. "Ten to one it'll clear up in an hour or so. And in the meantime we're pretty well off. There's a wireless* and lots of books."
>
> "Not for me," said Peter. "I'm going to explore in the house."
>
> Everyone agreed to this and that was how the adventures began. It was the sort of house that you never seem to come to the end of, and it was full of unexpected places. The first few doors they tried led only into spare bedrooms, as everyone had expected that they would; but soon they came to a very long room full of pictures and there they found a suit of <u>armor</u>; and after that was a room all hung with green, with a harp in one corner; and then came three steps down and five steps up, and then a kind of little upstairs hall and a door that led out onto a <u>balcony</u>, and then a whole series of rooms that led into each other and were lined with books — most of them very old books and some bigger than a Bible in a church. And shortly after that they looked into a room that was quite empty except for one big wardrobe; the sort that has a <u>looking-glass</u> in the door. There was nothing else in the room at all except a dead blue-bottle* on the window-sill.
>
> "Nothing there!" said Peter, and they all trooped out again — all except Lucy. She stayed behind because she thought it would be worth while trying the door of the wardrobe, even though she felt almost sure that it would be locked. To her surprise it opened quite easily, and two moth-balls dropped out.
>
> Looking into the inside, she saw several coats hanging up — mostly long fur coats.

*wireless - wireless radio / *blue-bottle - loud buzzing blowfly

(1) What is the main idea of the paragraph in gray? Check the best answer below.

( ) ⓐ That was how the adventures began.

( ) ⓑ The first few doors led only to spare bedrooms.

( ) ⓒ It was the sort of house that was full of unexpected places.

(2) Write the correct underlined word next to its definition below.

_____ a platform projecting from a wall

(3) Why did Lucy stay behind in the room with the wardrobe?

Lucy stayed behind because she thought _____

_____.

Read the passage. Then answer the questions below.

There was nothing Lucy liked so much as the smell and feel of fur. She immediately stepped into the wardrobe and got in among the coats and rubbed her face against them, leaving the door open, of course, because she knew that it is very foolish to shut oneself into any wardrobe. Soon she went further in and found that there was a second row of coats hanging up behind the first one. It was almost quite dark in there and she kept her arms stretched out in front of her so as not to bump her face into the back of the wardrobe. She took a step further in — then two or three steps — always expecting to feel the woodwork against the tips of her fingers. But she could not feel it.

"This must be a simply enormous wardrobe!" thought Lucy, going still further in and pushing the soft folds of the coats aside to make room for her. Then she noticed that there was something crunching under her feet. "I wonder is that more moth-balls?" she thought, stooping down to feel it with her hand. But instead of feeling the hard, smooth wood of the floor of the wardrobe, she felt something soft and powdery and extremely cold. "This is very queer," she said, and went on a step or two further.

Next moment she found that what was rubbing against her face and hands was no longer soft fur but something hard and rough and even prickly. "Why, it is just like the branches of trees!" exclaimed Lucy. And then she saw that there was a light ahead of her; not a few inches away where the back of the wardrobe ought to have been, but a long way off. Something cold and soft was falling on her. A moment later she found that she was standing in the middle of a wood at night-time with snow under her feet and snowflakes falling through the air.

(1) What was Lucy expecting to feel as she stepped further into the wardrobe?

Lucy was always expecting to feel the _____ of the back of the wardrobe against

_____.

(2) What did Lucy think as she went still further in?

Lucy thought that it must be a _____.

(3) What is the theme of this page? Check the best theme below.

(   ) ⓐ Exploration

(   ) ⓑ Snow

(   ) ⓒ Fur

(4) Where did Lucy find herself once she was no longer in the wardrobe?

Lucy found herself in the _____ at _____.

Wow, what a wardrobe!

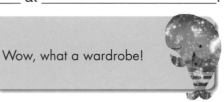

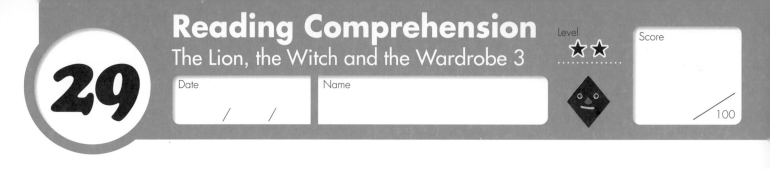

Reading Comprehension
The Lion, the Witch and the Wardrobe 3

Level ★★

Date   /   /

Name

Score

/100

1   Read the passage. Then answer the questions below.

Lucy felt a little frightened, but she felt very inquisitive and excited as well. She looked back over her shoulder and there, between the dark tree-trunks, she could still see the open doorway of the wardrobe and even catch a glimpse of the empty room from which she had set out. … It seemed to be still daylight there. "I can always get back if anything goes wrong," thought Lucy. She began to walk forward, crunch-crunch over the snow and through the wood toward the other light. In about ten minutes she reached it and found it was a lamp-post. As she stood looking at it, wondering why there was a lamp-post in the middle of a wood and wondering what to do next, she heard a pitter patter of feet coming toward her. And soon after that a very strange person stepped out from among the trees into the light of the lamp-post.

He was only a little taller than Lucy herself and he carried over his head an umbrella, white with snow. From the waist upward he was like a man, but his legs were shaped like a goat's (the hair on them was glossy black) and instead of feet he had goat's hoofs. He also had a tail, but Lucy did not notice this at first because it was neatly caught up over the arm that held the umbrella so as to keep it from trailing in the snow. He had a red woolen muffler round his neck and his skin was rather reddish too. He had a strange, but pleasant little face, with a short pointed beard and curly hair, and out of the hair there stuck two horns, one on each side of his forehead.

(1)   Check all the words below that describe Lucy. Use the underlined sentence as a guide.

30 points for completion

( ) ⓐ Curious ( ) ⓑ Angry ( ) ⓒ Energetic

( ) ⓓ Upset ( ) ⓔ Scared ( ) ⓕ Tired

(2)   Fill in the chart below about the description of the new character. Use the paragraph in gray as a guide.

3 points per question

Description of New Character	
From the waist up	He was ①_____
Legs	His legs were ②_____
Feet	Instead of feet he had ③_____
Neck	Round his neck was a ④_____
Face	He had a ⑤_____ face
Skin	His skin was ⑥_____
Beard and hair	He had a ⑦_____ and ⑧_____ hair
Forehead	There stuck ⑨_____, one on each ⑩_____

... WHAT LUCY FOUND THERE

"Good evening," said Lucy. But the Faun was so busy picking up its parcels that at first it did not reply. When it had finished it made her a little bow.

"Good evening, good evening," said the Faun. "Excuse me — I don't want to be inquisitive — but should I be right in thinking that you are a Daughter of Eve?"

"My name's Lucy," said she, not quite understanding him.

"But you are — forgive me — you are what they call a girl?" said the Faun.

"Of course I'm a girl," said Lucy.

"You are in fact Human?"

"Of course I'm human," said Lucy, still a little puzzled.

"To be sure, to be sure," said the Faun. "How stupid of me! But I've never seen a Son of Adam or a Daughter of Eve before. I am delighted. That is to say —" and then it stopped as if it had been going to say something it had not intended but had remembered in time. "Delighted, delighted," it went on. "Allow me to introduce myself. My name is Tumnus."

"I am very pleased to meet you, Mr. Tumnus," said Lucy.

"And may I ask, O Lucy Daughter of Eve," said Mr. Tumnus, "how you have come into Narnia?"

"Narnia? What's that?" said Lucy.

"This is the land of Narnia," said the Faun, "where we are now; all that lies between the lamp-post and the great castle of Cair Paravel on the eastern sea. And you — you have come from the wild woods of the west?"

"I — I got in through the wardrobe in the spare room," said Lucy.

"Ah!" said Mr. Tumnus in a rather melancholy voice, "if only I had worked harder at geography when I was a little Faun, I should no doubt know all about those strange countries."

Decide whether each of the following statements from the passage is a fact or an opinion.
Write "**F**" or "**O**" in the space provided.

(1) Of course I'm human. (   )

(2) How stupid of me! (   )

(3) This is the land of Narnia, where we are now; all that lies between the lamp-post and the great castle of Cair Paravel on the eastern sea. (   )

(4) I got in through the wardrobe in the spare room. (   )

(5) If only I had worked harder at geography when I was a little Faun, I should no doubt know all about those strange countries. (   )

Wow, in my opinion this is a strange country!

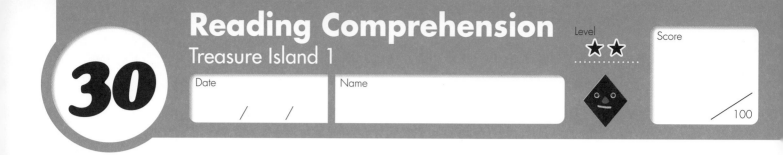

Reading Comprehension
Treasure Island 1

Level ★★

Date / /

Name

Score /100

1 Read the passage from *Treasure Island* by Robert Louis Stevenson, in which Jim talks of the captain that lived with his family. Then answer the questions below. 10 points per question

> It was not very long after this that there occurred the first of the mysterious events that rid us at last of the captain, though not, as you will see, of his affairs. It was a bitter cold winter, with long, hard frosts and heavy gales; and it was plain from the first that my poor father was little likely to see the spring. He sank daily, and my mother and I had all the inn upon our hands; and were kept busy enough, without paying much regard to our unpleasant guest.
>
> It was one January morning, very early — a pinching, frosty morning — the cove all grey with hoar-frost, the ripple lapping softly on the stones, the sun still low and only touching the hilltops and shining far to seaward. The captain had risen earlier than usual, and set out down the beach, his cutlass swinging under the broad skirts of the old blue coat, his brass telescope under his arm, his hat tilted back upon his head. I remember his breath hanging like smoke in his wake as he strode off, and the last sound I heard of him, as he turned the big rock, was a loud snort of indignation, as though his mind was still running upon Dr. Livesey.
>
> Well, mother was upstairs with father; and I was laying the breakfast table against the captain's return, when the parlour door opened, and a man stepped in on whom I had never set my eyes before.

(1) What sort of weather was there in the setting for this story?

It was a bitter _____, with _____.

(2) Who is the narrator referring to when he talks of their "unpleasant guest"? Check the correct answer below.

( ) ⓐ The father

( ) ⓑ Dr. Livesey

( ) ⓒ The captain

(3) How does the narrator describe the captain that morning?

The narrator describes the captain as having his cutlass _____

_____, with his _____

_____, and his _____.

(4) What does the narrator remember about the captain's breath?

The narrator remembers his breath _____.

(5) Was the man who entered the captain returning from his walk? Check the correct answer below.

( ) ⓐ Yes   ( ) ⓑ No

2 Read the passage. Then answer the questions below.

He was a pale, tallowy creature, wanting* two fingers of the left hand; and, though he wore a cutlass, he did not look much like a fighter. I had always my eye open for seafaring men, with one leg or two, and I remember this one puzzled me. He was not sailorly, and yet he had a smack of the sea about him too.

I asked him what was for his service*, and he said he would take rum; but as I was going out of the room to fetch it he sat down upon a table and motioned me to draw near. I paused where I was with my napkin in my hand.

"Come here, sonny," says he. "Come nearer here."

I took a step nearer.

"Is this here table for my mate Bill?" he asked, with a kind of leer.

I told him I did not know his mate Bill; and this was for a person who stayed in our house, whom we called the captain.

"Well," said he, "my mate Bill would be called the captain, as like as not. He has a cut on one cheek, and a mighty pleasant way with him, particularly in drink, has my mate Bill. We'll put it, for argument like, that your captain has a cut on one cheek — and we'll put it, if you like, that that cheek's the right one. Ah, well! I told you. Now, is my mate Bill in this here house?"

I told him he was out walking.

"Which way, sonny? Which way is he gone?"

And when I had pointed out the rock and told him how the captain was likely to return, and how soon, and answered a few other questions, "Ah," said he, "this'll be as good as drink to my mate Bill."

*wanting - lacking / *service - order

(1) Decide whether the following statements, taken from the description of the new character, are fact or opinion. Write "**F**" or "**O**" in the space provided.   8 points per question

① He was missing two fingers on his left hand.   (   )

② He wore a cutlass.   (   )

③ He did not look like a fighter.   (   )

④ He was not sailorly, but he had a smack of the sea about him too.   (   )

⑤ He ordered some rum.   (   )

(2) How does the new character describe the captain?   10 points

The new character says that the captain has a _____, and a

mighty _____.

Do you think this new character is the captain's friend?

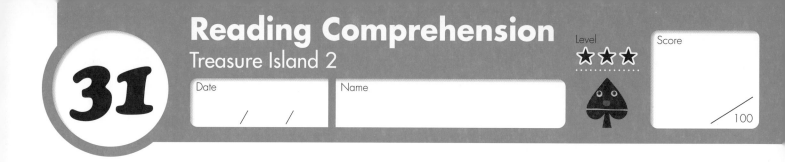

Reading Comprehension
Treasure Island 2

Level ★★★

Score

/100

Date   /   /

Name

1 Read the passage. Then answer the questions below.

10 points per question

> ...The stranger kept hanging about just outside the inn door, peering round the corner like a cat waiting for a mouse. Once I stepped out myself into the road, but he immediately called me back, and, as I did not obey quick enough for his fancy, a most horrible change came over his tallowy face, and he ordered me in, with an oath that made me jump.
>
> As soon as I was back again he returned to his former manner, half fawning, half sneering, patted me on the shoulder, told me I was a good boy, and he had taken quite a fancy to me. "I have a son of my own," said he, "as like you as two blocks, and he's all the pride of my 'art. But the great thing for boys is discipline, sonny — discipline. Now, if you had sailed along of Bill, you wouldn't have stood there to be spoke to twice — not you. That was never Bill's way, nor the way of sich* as sailed with him. And here, sure enough, is my mate Bill, with a spy-glass under his arm, bless his old 'art to be sure. You and me'll just go back into the parlour, sonny, and get behind the door, and we'll give Bill a little surprise — bless his 'art, I say again."
>
> So saying, the stranger backed along with me into the parlour, and put me behind him in the corner, so that we were both hidden by the open door. I was very uneasy and alarmed, as you may fancy, and it rather added to my fears to observe that the stranger was certainly frightened himself. He cleared the hilt of his cutlass and loosened the blade in the sheath; and all the time we were waiting there he kept swallowing as if he felt what we used to call a lump in the throat.

*sich - such

(1) What comparison does the narrator make to show how the stranger was waiting for the captain?

The narrator says that the stranger waited for the captain like a _____

_____ .

(2) What is the main idea of the second paragraph?

The main idea of the second paragraph is that the stranger told Jim he had _____

_____ to Jim but that boys need _____ .

(3) How did Jim feel as they waited for the captain in the parlour?

Jim was very _____ .

(4) How did the stranger feel as they waited for the captain in the parlour?

The stranger was certainly _____ .

(5) What did the stranger do in preparation for the captain's arrival?

The stranger cleared _____ and _____

_____ .

2 Read the passage. Then answer the questions below.

At last in strode the captain, slammed the door behind him, without looking to the right or left, and marched straight across the room to where his breakfast awaited him.

"Bill," said the stranger, in a voice that I thought he had tried to make bold and big.

The captain spun around on his heel and fronted us; all the brown had gone out of his face, and even his nose was blue; he had the look of a man who sees a ghost, or the evil one, or something worse, if anything can be; and, upon my word, I felt sorry to see him, all in a moment, turn so old and sick.

"Come, Bill, you know me; you know an old shipmate, Bill, surely," said the stranger.

The captain made a sort of gasp.

"Black Dog!" said he.

"And who else?" returned the other, getting more at his ease. "Black Dog as ever was, come for to see his old shipmate Billy, at the 'Admiral Benbow' inn. <u>Ah, Bill, Bill, we have seen a sight of times, us two, since I lost them two talons,</u>" holding up his mutilated hand.

"Now, look here," said the captain, "you've run me down; here I am; well, then, speak up; what is it?"

"That's you, Bill," returned Black Dog, "you're in the right of it, Billy. I'll have a glass of rum from this dear child here, as I've took such a liking to; and we'll sit down, if you please, and talk square, like old shipmates."

When I returned with the rum, they were already seated on either side of the captain's breakfast table — Black Dog next to the door, and sitting sideways, so as to have one eye on his old shipmate, and one, as I thought, on his retreat.

(1) How did the stranger greet the captain?   10 points

The stranger greeted the captain with a voice that Jim thought _____

_____.

(2) What was the captain's initial reaction to seeing the stranger?   10 points

All the _____, and even _____

_____ ; he had the look of a man _____.

(3) How did Black Dog sit as he spoke to the captain?   10 points

Black Dog sat _____ so he could have one eye _____,

and one _____.

(4) Put a check next to the sentence below that means the same as the underlined sentence in the passage.

                                                                                                  20 points

(   ) ⓐ Black Dog and the captain have a long history.

(   ) ⓑ Black Dog and the captain have hunted birds together.

(   ) ⓒ Black Dog has seen the captain lose talons.

I want a nickname like Black Dog!

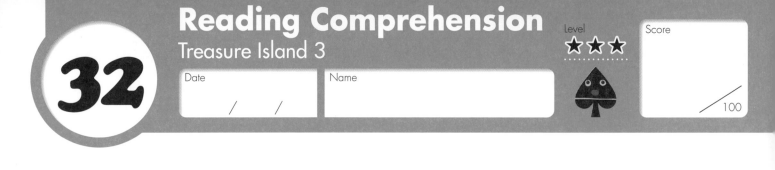

Reading Comprehension
Treasure Island 3

Level ★★★

Date / /

Name

Score /100

32

1 Read the passage. Then answer the questions below.   10 points per question

He bade me go, and leave the door wide open. "None of your keyholes for me, sonny," he said; and I left them together and retired into the bar.

For a long time, though I certainly did my best to listen, I could hear nothing but a low gabbling; but at last the voices began to grow higher, and I could pick up a word or two, mostly oaths, from the captain.

"No, no, no, no; and an end of it!" he cried once. And again, "If it comes to swinging, swing all, say I."

Then all of a sudden there was a tremendous explosion of oaths and other noises — the chair and table went over in a lump, a clash of steel followed, and then a cry of pain, and the next instant I saw Black Dog in full flight, and the captain hotly pursuing, both with drawn cutlasses, and the former streaming blood from the left shoulder. Just at the door, the captain aimed at the fugitive one last tremendous cut, which would certainly have split him to the chine* had it not been intercepted by our big signboard of Admiral Benbow. You may see the notch on the lower side of the frame to this day.

That blow was the last of the battle. Once out upon the road, Black Dog, in spite of his wound, <u>showed a wonderful clean pair of heels</u>, and disappeared over the edge of the hill in half a minute. The captain, for his part, stood staring at the signboard like a bewildered man. Then he passed his hand over his eyes several times, and at last turned back into the house.

"Jim," says he, "rum;" and as he spoke, he reeled a little, and caught himself with one hand against the wall.

*chine - backbone or spine

(1) What could Jim hear when the captain and Black Dog were talking?

For a long time, he could hear nothing _____ , but once the voices

got louder, he could _____ , mostly _____

_____ .

(2) What is the best theme for the paragraph in gray? Check the correct answer.

(   ) ⓐ Explosion   (   ) ⓑ Conflict   (   ) ⓒ Pain

(3) What saved Black Dog from one last tremendous cut?

Black Dog would have received one last tremendous cut if it had not been _____

_____ the _____ .

(4) Put a check next to the sentence below that means the same as the underlined sentence in the passage.

(   ) ⓐ Black Dog had nice shoes.

(   ) ⓑ Black Dog ran quickly.

(   ) ⓒ Black Dog stole some shoes.

Read the passage. Then answer the questions below.

"Are you hurt?" cried I.

"Rum," he repeated. "I must get away from here. Rum! Rum!"

I ran to fetch it, but I was quite unsteadied by all that had fallen out, and I broke one glass and fouled the tap, and while I was still getting in my own way, I heard a loud fall in the parlour, and, running in, beheld the captain lying full length upon the floor. At the same instant my mother, alarmed by the cries and fighting, came running downstairs to help me. Between us **we** raised his head. He was breathing very loud and hard; but his eyes were closed, and his face a horrible colour.

"Dear, deary me," cried my mother, "what a disgrace upon the house! And your poor father sick!"

In the meantime, we had no idea what to do to help the captain, nor any other thought but that he had got his death-hurt in the scuffle with the stranger. I got the rum, to be sure, and tried to put it down his throat, but his teeth were tightly shut, and his jaws as strong as iron. It was a happy relief for us when the door opened and Doctor Livesey came in, on his visit to my father.

"Oh, doctor," we cried, "what shall we do? Where is he wounded?"

"Wounded? A fiddle-stick's end!" said the doctor. "No more wounded than you or I. The man has had a stroke, as I warned him. Now, Mrs. Hawkins, just you run upstairs to your husband, and tell him, if possible, nothing about it. For my part, I must do my best to save this fellow's trebly* worthless life; and Jim here will get me a basin."

*trebly - three times as much, triply

(1) How was the narrator feeling as he went to get the rum?

The narrator was feeling quite _____ by _____.

(2) Who does the "we" in bold refer to?

The "we" refers to _____.

(3) How was the captain described at the moment they raised his head?

The captain was _____; but his _____

_____, and his _____.

(4) What happened when Jim tried to give the captain some rum?

Jim couldn't give him rum because his _____, and

_____.

(5) What happened to the captain?

The captain _____.

I wonder what Black Dog said!

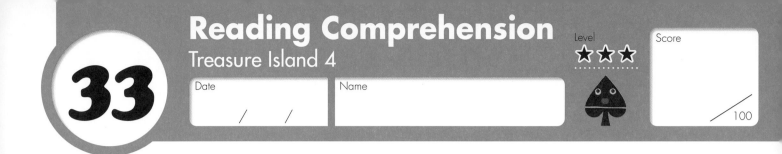

Reading Comprehension
Treasure Island 4

Level ★★★

Date   /   /

Name

Score
/100

1   Read the passage. Then answer the questions below.

When I got back with the basin, the doctor had already ripped up the captain's sleeve, and exposed his great sinewy arm. It was tattooed in several places. "Here's luck," "A fair wind," and "Billy Bones his fancy," were very neatly and clearly executed on the forearm; and up near the shoulder there was a sketch of a gallows and a man hanging from it — done, as I thought, with great spirit.

"Prophetic,*" said the doctor, touching this picture with his finger. "And now, Master Billy Bones, if that be your name, we'll have a look at the colour of your blood. Jim," he said, "are you afraid of blood?"

"No sir," said I.

"Well, then," said he, "you hold the basin." …

A great deal of blood was taken before the captain opened his eyes and looked mistily about him. First he recognized the doctor with an unmistakable frown; then his glance fell upon me, and he looked relieved. But suddenly his colour changed, and he tried to raise himself, crying:

"Where's Black Dog?"

"There is no Black Dog here," said the doctor, "except what you have on your own back. You have been drinking rum; you have had a stroke, precisely as I told you; and I have just, very much against my own will, dragged you head-foremost out of the grave. Now, Mr. Bones —"

"That's not my name," he interrupted.

"Much I care," returned the doctor.

*prophetic - related to the prediction of future events

(1)   Decide whether the following statements with information taken from the passage are fact or opinion. Write "**F**" or "**O**" in the space provided.

8 points per question

① The arm was tattooed in several places. (   )

② The sketch of the man hanging from the gallows was done in great spirit. (   )

③ The doctor touched a tattoo. (   )

④ The captain looked relieved. (   )

⑤ Blood was taken. (   )

(2)   Was the captain happy to see the doctor?

10 points

_____, he recognized the doctor with an _____.

Read the passage. Then answer the questions below.

"It's the name of a buccaneer of my acquaintance, and I call you by it for the sake of shortness, and what I have to say to you is this: one glass of rum won't kill you, but if you take one you'll take another and another, and I stake my wig if you don't break off short, you'll die — do you understand that? — die, and go to your own place, like the man in the Bible. Come, now, make an effort. I'll help you to your bed for once."

Between us, with much trouble, (a) <u>we managed to hoist him upstairs</u>, and laid him on his bed, where his head fell back on the pillow, as if he were almost fainting.

"Now, mind you," said the doctor, "I clear my conscience — the name of rum for you is death." And with that he went off to see my father, taking me with him by the arm.

"This is nothing," he said, as soon as he had closed the door. "I have drawn blood enough to keep him quiet a while; he should lie for a week where he is — that is the best thing for him and you; but another stroke would settle him."

3. THE BLACK SPOT

About noon I stopped at the captain's door with some cooling drinks and medicines. (b) <u>He was lying very much as we had left him, only a little higher, and he seemed both weak and excited.</u>

"Jim," he said, "you're the only one here that's worth anything; and you know I've always been good to you. Never a month but I've given you a silver fourpenny for yourself. And now you see, mate, I'm pretty low, and deserted by all; and, Jim, you'll bring me one noggin of rum, now won't you, matey?"

(c) <u>"The doctor —" I began.</u>
But he broke in cursing the doctor, in a feeble voice, but heartily.

(1) Write the letter from each underlined section in the passage that corresponds to each story element listed below.

10 points per question

① An action that furthers the plot: (   )

② Something said by the main character: (   )

③ A description of the secondary character: (   )

(2) Do you think the captain will heed the doctor's advice?   20 points

_____

_____ .

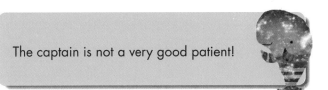

The captain is not a very good patient!

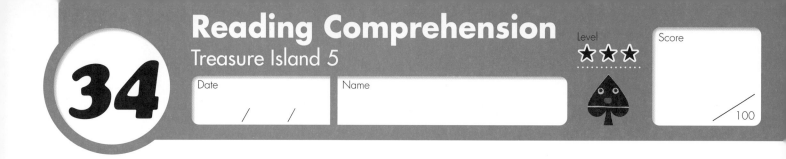

Reading Comprehension
Treasure Island 5

Level ★★★

1 Read the passage. Then answer the questions below.

10 points per question

> …"Look, Jim, how my fingers fidget," he continued in the pleading tone. "I can't keep 'em still, not I. I haven't had a drop this blessed day. That doctor's a fool, I tell you. If I don't have a drain o' rum, Jim, I'll have the horrors; I seen some on 'em already. … Your doctor hisself said one glass wouldn't hurt me. I'll give you a golden guinea for a noggin, Jim."
>
> He was growing more and more excited, and this alarmed me for my father, who was very low that day, and needed quiet; besides, I was reassured by the doctor's words, now quoted to me, and rather offended by the offer of a bribe.
>
> "I want none of your money," said I, "but what you owe my father. I'll get you one glass, and no more."
>
> When I brought it to him, he seized it greedily and drank it out.
>
> "Ay, ay," said he, "that's some better, sure enough. And now, matey, did that doctor say how long I was to lie here in this old berth*?"
>
> "A week at least," said I.
>
> "Thunder!" he cried. "A week! I can't do that: they'd have the black spot on me by then. The lubbers* is going about to get the wind of me this blessed moment; lubbers as couldn't keep what they got, and want to nail what is another's. Is that seamanly behaviour, now, I want to know? But I'm a saving soul. I never wasted good money of mine, nor lost it neither; and I'll trick 'em again. I'm not afraid on 'em. I'll shake out another reef*, matey, and daddle* 'em again."

*berth - a place to sit or sleep, especially on a ship
*lubber - clumsy person, from 'landlubber,' which means someone who has no sea experience
*shake out another reef - to let out more sail in order to go faster / *daddle - cheat

(1) Why was the main character alarmed by the captain's excitement?

Jim was alarmed for his _____, who needed _____.

(2) Why was the main character offended by the captain's words?

Jim was offended by _____.

(3) When Jim brought the captain the rum, what did the captain do?

The captain _____ the rum _____ and _____.

(4) What is the theme of the paragraph in gray? Check the best answer below.

( ) ⓐ The captain is a trickster.

( ) ⓑ Someone is after the captain's money.

( ) ⓒ The captain is after the black spot.

( ) ⓓ Someone is a better seaman than the captain.

2 Read the passage. Then answer the questions below.

12 points per question

As he was thus speaking, he had risen from bed with great difficulty, holding to my shoulder with a grip that almost made me cry out, and moving his legs like so much dead weight. His words, spirited as they were in meaning, contrasted sadly with the weakness of the voice in which they were uttered. He paused when he had got into a sitting position on the edge.

"That doctor's done me," he murmured. "My ears is singing. Lay me back."

Before I could do much to help him he had fallen back again to his former place, where he lay for a while silent.

"Jim," he said at length, "you saw that seafaring man today?"

"Black Dog?" I asked.

"Ah! Black Dog," said he. "He's a bad 'un; but there's worse that put him on. Now, if I can't get away nohow, and they tip me the black spot, mind you, it's my old sea-chest they're after; you get on a horse — you can, can't you? Well then, you get on a horse, and go to — well, yes, I will! — to that eternal doctor swab, and tell him to pipe all hands* — magistrates and sich — and he'll lay 'em aboard at the Admiral Benbow — all old Flint's crew, man and boy, all on 'em that's left. I was first mate, I was, old Flint's first mate, and I'm the on'y one as knows the place. He gave it to me …when he lay a-dying, like as if I was to now, you see. But you won't peach* unless they get the black spot on me, or unless you see that Black Dog again, or a seafaring man with one leg, Jim — him above all."

"But what is the black spot, Captain?" I asked.

"That's a summons, mate. I'll tell you if they get that. But you keep your weather-eye open, Jim, and I'll share with you equals, upon my honour."

pipe all hands - call men together / *peach* - inform against

(1) What contrasted sadly with the captain's spirited words?

The _____ of the captain's _____ contrasted sadly with the captain's spirited words.

(2) Did Jim help the captain back onto the bed? Check the right answer below.

( ) ⓐ Yes   ( ) ⓑ No

(3) What did the captain think everyone was after?

The captain thought everyone was after his old _____.

(4) Who gave the captain his treasure? When?

Old _____ gave the captain his treasure as _____.

(5) What did the captain promise the narrator if he kept his weather-eye open?

The captain promised the narrator that he would _____ him _____ if he helped.

You have to read the book to find out where the treasure is!

69

Review

35

Level ★★

Date / /

Name

Score

/100

1 Read the passage below, which continues *The Princess & the Goblin*. Then answer the questions while looking at the corresponding place in the passage.

10 points per question

'That's *my* name!' cried the princess.

'I know that. I let you have mine. I haven't got your name. You've got mine.'

'How can that be?' asked the princess, bewildered. 'I've always had my name.'

'Your papa, the king, asked me if I had any objection to your having it; and, of course, I hadn't. ⓐ I let you have **it** with pleasure.'

'It was very kind of you to give me your name — and such a pretty one,' said the princess.

'Oh, not so very kind!' said the old lady. 'A name is one of those things one can give away and keep all the same. I have a good many such things. Wouldn't you like to know who I am, child?'

'Yes, that I should — very much.'

'I'm your great-great-grandmother,' said the lady.

'What's that?' asked the princess.

'I'm your father's mother's father's mother.'

'Oh dear! I can't understand that,' said the princess.

'I dare say not. I didn't expect you would. But that's no reason why I shouldn't say it.'

'Oh no!' answered the princess.

'I will explain it all to you when you are older,' the lady went on. 'But you will be able to understand this much now: I came here to take care of you.'

'Is it long since you came? Was it yesterday? Or was it today, because it was so wet that I couldn't get out?'

'I've been here ever since you came yourself.'

'What a long time!' said the princess. ⓑ 'I don't remember **it** at all.'

(1) What does the "it" refer to in sentence ⓐ ? Rewrite the sentence.

I let you have _____ with pleasure.

(2) Interpretation: "A name is one of those things one can give away and keep all the same" means that both the _____ and her great-great-grandmother can share the same _____.

(3) Interpretation: "But that's no reason why I shouldn't say it," means that the lady thought that the princess wouldn't _____ what a _____ was, but that she would tell her anyway.

(4) What does the "it" refer to in sentence ⓑ ? Check the right answer.

( ) ⓐ The day when the lady gave her name to the princess.

( ) ⓑ The day the princess arrived at the country house.

( ) ⓒ Yesterday.

2 Read the passage. Then decide whether each of the following sentences is a fact or an opinion. Write "**F**" or "**O**" in the space provided.

10 points per question

'No. I suppose not.'

'But I never saw you before.'

'No. But you shall see me again.'

'Do you live in this room always?'

'I don't sleep in it. I sleep on the opposite side of the landing. I sit here most of the day.'

'I shouldn't like it. My nursery is much prettier. You must be a queen too, if you are my great big grandmother.'

'Yes, I am a queen.'

'Where is your crown, then?'

'In my bedroom.'

'I should like to see it.'

'You shall some day — not today.'

'I wonder why nursie never told me.'

'Nursie doesn't know. She never saw me.'

'But somebody knows that you are in the house?'

'No; nobody.'

'How do you get your dinner, then?'

'I keep a poultry — of a sort.'

'Where do you keep them?'

'I will show you.'

'And who makes the chicken broth for you?'

'I never kill any of my chickens.'

'Then I can't understand.'

'What did you have for breakfast this morning?' asked the lady.

'Oh! I had bread and milk, and an egg — I dare say you eat their eggs.'

'Yes, that's it. I eat their eggs.'

'Is that what makes your hair so white?'

'No, my dear. It's old age. I am very old.'

(1)   I never saw you before.   (   )

(2)   I don't sleep in it.   (   )

(3)   My nursery is much prettier.   (   )

(4)   I should like to see it.   (   )

(5)   I never kill any of my chickens.   (   )

(6)   I had bread and milk, and an egg.   (   )

What a strange lady!

71

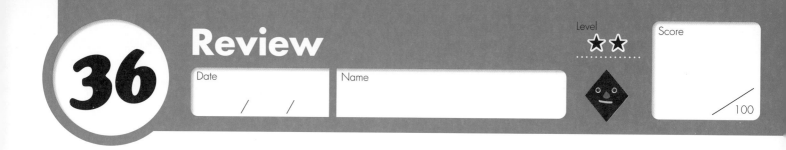

1 Read the passage below, which continues *The Princess & the Goblin*. Then answer the questions below.

10 points per question

> 'I thought so. Are you fifty?'
> 'Yes — more than that.'
> 'Are you a hundred?'
> 'Yes — more than that. I am too old for you to guess. Come and see my chickens.'
> Again she stopped her spinning. She rose, took the princess by the hand, led her out of the room, and opened the door opposite the stair. The princess expected to see a lot of hens and chickens, but instead of that, she saw the blue sky first, and then the roofs of the house, with a multitude of the loveliest pigeons, mostly white, but of all colours, walking about, making bows to each other, and talking a language she could not understand. She clapped her hands with delight, and up rose such a flapping of wings that she in her turn was startled.
> 'You've frightened my poultry,' said the old lady, smiling.
> 'And they've frightened me,' said the princess, smiling too. 'But what very nice poultry! Are the eggs nice?'
> 'Yes, very nice.'
> 'What a small egg-spoon you must have! Wouldn't it be better to keep hens, and get bigger eggs?'
> 'How should I feed them, though?'
> 'I see,' said the princess. 'The pigeons feed themselves. They've got wings.'
> 'Just so. If they couldn't fly, I couldn't eat their eggs.'
> 'But how do you get at the eggs? Where are their nests?'
> The lady took hold of a little loop of string in the wall at the side of the door and, lifting a shutter, showed a great many pigeon-holes with nests, some with young ones and some with eggs in them. The birds came in at the other side, and she took out the eggs on this side.

(1) Describe the new setting that the lady shows the princess.

Instead of a lot of _____, the princess saw _____

first, and then the _____.

(2) How did the main character frighten the poultry?

The _____ frightened the poultry when she _____

_____.

(3) What did the new character think about the eggs?

The _____ thought the eggs were _____.

(4) Where were the pigeons' nests?

The pigeons' nests were under a _____ inside a great many _____.

© Kumon Publishing Co., Ltd.

2 Read the passage. Then answer the questions below.

She closed it again quickly, lest the young ones should be frightened.

'Oh, what a nice way!' cried the princess. 'Will you give me an egg to eat? I'm rather hungry.'

'I will some day, but now you must go back, or nursie will be miserable about you. I dare say she's looking for you everywhere.'

'Except here,' answered the princess. ⓐ'Oh, how surprised she will be when I tell her about my great big grand-grand-mother!'

'Yes, that she will!' said the old lady with a curious smile. 'Mind you tell her all about it exactly.'

'That I will. Please will you take me back to her?'

'I can't go all the way, but I will take you to the top of the stair, and then you must run down quite fast into your own room.'

The little princess put her hand in the old lady's, who, looking this way and that, brought her to the top of the first stair, and thence to the bottom of the second, and did not leave her till she saw her half-way down the third. When she heard the cry of her nurse's pleasure at finding her, she turned and walked up the stairs again, very fast indeed for such a very great grandmother, and ⓑsat down to her spinning with another strange smile on her sweet old face.

ⓒAbout this spinning of hers I will tell you more another time.

Guess what she was spinning.

(1) Write the letter from each underlined section in the passage that corresponds to each story element listed below.

12 points per question

① The narrator makes a comment on the story. ( )

② The main character makes a prediction. ( )

③ An action that furthers the plot. ( )

(2) What is the main idea of the passage in gray? 12 points

The old lady helped the princess until she heard _____

_____.

(3) What is the best theme for this passage? Check the best answer below. 12 points

( ) ⓐ Mystery   ( ) ⓑ Pigeons   ( ) ⓒ Sadness

Well done. You're a star!

1 Vocabulary
pp 2, 3

1 (1) ① secrecy ② site ③ illegible
④ antique ⑤ inspected ⑥ genuine
(2) ① taking chances on anyone else waking up
② person in town who she thought could help

2 (1) inspected the contents of every drawer
(2) a matter of secrecy
(3) the story was genuine
(4) on the map was illegible
(5) the day walking through the trails and finally

2 Vocabulary
pp 4, 5

1 (1) ① strategy ② regulations ③ smuggling
④ consider ⑤ mechanism
(2) ① to the town
② on a rock in the shade
③ might belong to the town

2 (1) to dig up the buried treasure
(2) learn about the town's regulations
(3) smuggling protected wildlife away from
(4) mechanism that could carry up the box of treasure / harming any of the nearby plants

3 Vocabulary
pp 6, 7

1 (1) ① combination ② superb ③ convey
④ matrimony ⑤ jovial ⑥ incompetent
(2) ① two puppets would dance along with the troupe
② partners lifted them so high

2 (1) dancing continued to be superb
(2) the crowd conveyed its amazement with gasps and applause
(3) part of the act / a jovial leap in response
(4) The incompetent puppeteer
(5) a combination of all three reasons

4 Vocabulary
pp 8, 9

1 (1) ① Caverns
② limestone
③ crevices
④ subterranean
⑤ formations
⑥ treacherous
(2) ① about the life of prehistoric man
② crystals on earth are inside

2 (1) the formations on the
(2) it is a hole that drops straight down into the sea
(3) difficult / poisonous gases
(4) subterranean / limestone / above the sea

5 Vocabulary Review
pp 10, 11

1 (1) combination
(2) crevices
(3) nautical
(4) genuine
(5) formations
(6) incompetent

2 (1) consider
(2) illegible
(3) treacherous
(4) valuables
(5) convey
(6) mechanism

3 (1) JOVIAL
(2) SUBTERRANEAN
(3) MATRIMONY
(4) SMUGGLING
(5) STRATEGY
(6) REGULATIONS
(7) VARIETY
(8) ANTIQUE

6 Main Idea, Theme & Supporting Details   pp 12,13

1 (1) ① conserve water
② most important substances
③ limited supply
④ Droughts
⑤ Polluted

(2) ① D ② C ③ A ④ B

2 (1) ⓑ

(2) ① C ② A ③ B

(3) Ways to Conserve Water at Home

7 Main Idea, Theme & Supporting Details   pp 14,15

1 (1) ⓑ

(2) A

(3) capable hunters

2 (1) hunters

(2) (groups called) prides

(3) roar to communicate

8 Main Idea, Theme & Supporting Details   pp 16,17

1 (1) ⓒ

(2) B

(3) sport

2 (1) ⓐ

(2) ⓑ

(3) ⓒ

9 Main Idea, Theme & Supporting Details   pp 18,19

1 (1) ⓑ

(2) ⓒ

(3) transcontinental railroad changed the United States of America

2 (1) ⓒ

(2) ⓑ

(3) ⓐ

10 Vocabulary Review   pp 20,21

1 (1) capable

(2) management

(3) conserve

(4) merchant

(5) terrain

(6) isolated

2 (1) source

(2) establish

(3) crucial

(4) convenient

(5) correspondence

(6) occurred

3 (1) POPULATION

(2) BREAKTHROUGHS

(3) REQUIRED

(4) OBVIOUS

(5) FATIGUE

(6) DROUGHT

(7) TERRITORY

(8) UTILIZE

11 Interpreting Text   pp 22,23

1 (1) ① pictures and sketches
② Calvin's
③ asked Calvin to install some new software on her computer

(2) good with computers

2 (1) the program

(2) Calvin

(3) mosaic option

(4) Looking in a mirror

(5) his picture

(12) Interpreting Text
pp 24, 25

1 (1) cultural and entertainment centers
(2) many cities in Europe and the Middle East
(3) improved transportation
(4) People in cities

2 (1) the world's resources
(2) Mumbai, India, and Shanghai, China
(3) Improvements in transportation
(4) people live in city suburbs

(13) Interpreting Text
pp 26, 27

1 (1) tribes (2) lifestyle
(3) span (4) hostile
(5) culture (6) uprooted
(7) bleak (8) diet

2 blaming / uprooting

3 (1) similar / different
(2) it is not unusual
(3) group / spread / continuous
(4) working / occupations

(14) Interpreting Text
pp 28, 29

1 (1) main food source
(2) reindeer / supplies
(3) short-term, hunting-ground / the winter
(4) cut out / compact

2 (1) sounds
(2) single language group

3 become acquainted / to demonstrate who is the stronger of the two

(15) Interpreting Text
pp 30, 31

1 (1) Inuit to abandon their nomadic hunting lifestyle and traditional utensils
(2) declined / diminished feature

2 (1) up their nomadic lifestyle / lands were split
(2) ⓑ

(16) Vocabulary Review
pp 32, 33

1 (1) linguistics
(2) hostile
(3) merged
(4) migrate
(5) utensil
(6) seize

2 (1) provisions
(2) metropolis
(3) peripheral
(4) dwellings
(5) necessities
(6) nomad

3 (1) LIFESTYLE
(2) TRADITIONALLY
(3) EXCEEDED
(4) ACQUAINTED
(5) HECTIC
(6) ACCEPTANCE
(7) INFLUENCES
(8) BLEAK

(17) Fact & Opinion
pp 34, 35

1 (1) O
(2) F
(3) O
(4) F

2 forests / Tibet / bamboo

3 (1) "The Cloisters" / lovely outdoor
(2) manufacturers / cars / domestic

4 (1) F
(2) O
(3) O
(4) O
(5) F

18 Fact & Opinion
pp 36, 37

1 (1) Vostok 6 / cosmonaut / woman
(2) Guernica / protest / artist

2 (1) F
(2) F
(3) O
(4) O
(5) F

3 (1) front / prey / four
(2) relaxing / sparkling water / buoyancy

4 (1) bordered by North Korea
(2) was torn down in 1989
(3) are not fashionable
(4) is huge and interesting

19 Fact & Opinion
pp 38, 39

1 Latin American / samba / dances

2 (1) uses long metal clubs to hit a small white ball
(2) are marvels of engineering
(3) the world's tallest animal
(4) the most famous structure in France

3 (1) ⓑ
(2) fiber optics

4 (1) cables / Massachusetts / circuits
(2) light / bundles / fax

20 Fact & Opinion
pp 40, 41

1 (1) ⓑ
(2) supernatural and were linked to black magic

2 (1) ⓒ
(2) simple compound found in millipedes and peach pits
(3) toxicology / benefits / quinine

21 Vocabulary Review
pp 42, 43

1 (1) approximately
(2) buoyant
(3) circuits
(4) situated
(5) concentrated
(6) picturesque

2 (1) nuisance
(2) region
(3) toxins
(4) delicacy
(5) vast
(6) medieval

3 (1) REVOLUTIONIZED
(2) SUPERNATURAL
(3) PROCESS
(4) INHABITANTS
(5) INNOVATION
(6) FUNCTIONING
(7) VENOM
(8) INFLUENCE

22 Story Elements
pp 44, 45

1 (1) princess (Irene)
(2) fair and pretty / eyes like two bits of the night sky / with a star dissolved in the blue
(3) house, half castle, half farmhouse / mountain

2 (1) hollow places / caverns / winding ways
(2) race of beings / refuge in the subterranean caverns / at night
(3) had all disappeared from the face of the country
(4) night / showed themselves / to many people at once

23 Story Elements
pp 46, 47

1 (1) ① hideous
　　② knowledge and cleverness
　　③ grew in mischief
(2) heartily / ancestral / descendants of the king who had caused their expulsion

2 (1) about eight years old
(2) wet day / covered with mist
(3) tired / tired that even her toys could no longer amuse her
(4) artist / draw

24 Story Elements
pp 48, 49

1 (1) miserable
(2) tumbles / runs out of the door
(3) third flight / doors / each side
(4) silent / with nobody in them / great trampling noise on the roof

2 (1) that she had lost the way back
(2) herself on the floor / burst into a wailing cry
(3) ① ⓑ　② ⓐ　③ ⓒ

25 Story Elements
pp 50, 51

1 (1) gentle / monotonous
(2) of a very happy bee that had found a rich well of honey in some globular flower
(3) ① smooth and white
　　② loose
　　③ wise

2 (1) ⓒ
(2) ⓐ
(3) ⓓ
(4) ⓑ
(5) ⓔ

26 Vocabulary Review
pp 52, 53

1 (1) ore
(2) wailing
(3) theme
(4) resolved
(5) ravine
(6) cherish

2 (1) monotonous
(2) eaves
(3) subterranean
(4) ludicrous
(5) ancestors
(6) expulsion

3 (1) GROTESQUE
(2) DESCENDANTS
(3) NARRATOR
(4) BEWILDERED
(5) CHARACTER
(6) PLOT
(7) TORMENTING
(8) SETTING

27 Reading Comprehension
pp 54, 55

1 (1) the war because of the air-raids
(2) a very old man with shaggy white hair which grew over most of his face
(3) odd-looking
(4) let / do anything

2 (1) ten minutes' walk / to that dining room / amount of stairs and passages in between
(2) larger house than she had ever been in before / passages and rows of doors leading into empty rooms
(3) you looked out of the window / mountains nor the woods nor even the stream in the garden

28 Reading Comprehension

28 **Reading Comprehension**　　pp 56,57

1 (1) ⓒ
　(2) balcony
　(3) it would be worth while trying the door of the wardrobe

2 (1) woodwork / the tips of her fingers
　(2) simply enormous wardrobe
　(3) ⓐ
　(4) middle of a wood / night-time

29 **Reading Comprehension**　　pp 58,59

1 (1) ⓐ, ⓒ, ⓔ
　(2) ① like a man
　　　② shaped like a goat's
　　　③ goat's hoofs
　　　④ red woolen muffler
　　　⑤ strange, but pleasant little
　　　⑥ rather reddish
　　　⑦ short pointed beard
　　　⑧ curly
　　　⑨ two horns
　　　⑩ side of his forehead

2 (1) F　(2) O　(3) F　(4) F　(5) O

30 **Reading Comprehension**　　pp 60,61

1 (1) cold winter / long, hard frosts and heavy gales
　(2) ⓒ
　(3) swinging under the broad skirts of the old blue coat / brass telescope under his arm / hat tilted back upon his head
　(4) hanging like smoke in his wake
　(5) ⓑ

2 (1) ① F　② F　③ O　④ O　⑤ F
　(2) cut on one cheek / pleasant way with him

31 **Reading Comprehension**　　pp 62,63

1 (1) cat waiting for a mouse
　(2) taken quite a fancy / discipline
　(3) uneasy and alarmed
　(4) frightened himself
　(5) the hilt of his cutlass / loosened the blade in the sheath

2 (1) he had tried to make bold and big
　(2) brown had gone out of his face / his nose was blue / who sees a ghost
　(3) sideways / on his old shipmate / on his retreat
　(4) ⓐ

32 **Reading Comprehension**　　pp 64,65

1 (1) but a low gabbling / pick up a word or two / oaths, from the captain
　(2) ⓑ
　(3) intercepted by / big signboard of Admiral Benbow
　(4) ⓑ

2 (1) unsteadied / all that had fallen out
　(2) (the narrator) Jim and his mother
　(3) breathing very loud and hard / eyes were closed / face a horrible colour
　(4) teeth were tightly shut / his jaws (were) as strong as iron
　(5) had a stroke

33 **Reading Comprehension**　　pp 66,67

1 (1) ① F　② O　③ F　④ O　⑤ F
　(2) No / unmistakable frown

2 (1) ① ⓐ　② ⓒ　③ ⓑ
　(2) No, I don't think the captain will heed the doctor's advice (possible answer)

(34) Reading Comprehension   pp 68,69

1 (1) father / quiet
   (2) the offer of a bribe
   (3) seized / greedily / drank it out
   (4) ⓑ

2 (1) weakness / voice
   (2) ⓑ
   (3) sea-chest
   (4) Flint / he lay a-dying
   (5) share with / equals

(35) Review   pp 70,71

1 (1) my name
   (2) princess / name
   (3) understand / great-great-grandmother
   (4) ⓑ

2 (1) F
   (2) F
   (3) O
   (4) O
   (5) F
   (6) F

(36) Review   pp 72,73

1 (1) hens and chickens / the blue sky / roofs of the house
   (2) princess / clapped her hands with delight
   (3) (old) lady 〔great-great-grandmother〕 / very nice
   (4) shutter / pigeon-holes

2 (1) ① ⓒ ② ⓐ ③ ⓑ
   (2) the cry of her nurse's pleasure at finding her
   (3) ⓐ